# GWLADYS STREET'S
# HALL of FAME
™

## ESTABLISHED 1998

ACCEPT NO IMITATIONS

GWLADYS STREET

**D H FRANCE**

## DEDICATION ...

To the memory of
Peter Farrell (1922-1999)

## THE AUTHOR ...

David France is a management consultant based in Texas. He specialises in the re-structuring of companies and organisations world-wide. Dr France made his first pilgrimage to Goodison Park in 1957.

His other Everton books include:
T*offee Cards - The Tobacco Years* (ISBN 1-874799-05-9)
*Toffee Pages - The Post-War Years* (ISBN 1-874799-06-7)
*Gwladys Street's Hall of Fame* (ISBN 1-874799-09-1)
*Gwladys Street's Hall of Fame - Edition II* (ISBN 1-874799-10-5)

## ACKNOWLEDGEMENTS ...

Many people have given their time and energy to produce this book.

The author would like to express his sincere appreciation to Tom Cannon, Len Capeling, Tommy Clinton, Garry Doolan, John Dwyer, Tommy Eglington, Graham Ennis, Elizabeth France, Brian Harris, Derek Hatton, Dave Hickson, Mike Hughes, Norman Jones, TG Jones, John Keith, Bill Kenwright, Roger Kenyon, Ian MacDonald, Duncan McKenzie, Philip McNulty, Steve Milne, Shea Neary, Jimmy O'Neill, Phil Pellow, Fred Pickering, Kevin Ratcliffe, Mike Royden, Ian Rush, Steve Seargeant, Graeme Sharp, Neville Smith, Gordon Watson, Gordon West, Graham Wilson and Alex Young for their assistance.

He would like to thank the panel of Evertonians who reviewed the 1999 ballot results:
Norman Dainty - Everton Shareholders' Association
Andy Hunter - sports writer, *The Evertonian*
Jim King - Everton Supporters' (Goodison) Club
Brian Labone - former-player, Everton & England
Steven Milne - Merseyside Football Programmes
George Orr - author, *Everton In The Sixties*
David Prentice - sports writer, *Liverpool Echo*
Phil Redmond - co-editor, *When Skies Are Grey*
Harry Ross - vicar, St Luke the Evangelist
Mark Staniford - editor, *Speke From The Harbour*

Also he is indebted to Barry Hewitt and Ian Ross for validating the players' biographical records, Peter King and Dave Sheehan for their drawings, Roger McGough for his words and Jonathan Rimmer for his creative inputs.

Last but not least, he is grateful to Howard Kendall for the glory years and much more.

# FOREWORD BY HOWARD KENDALL

When I returned to Goodison for the second time as manager
I explained that you can have love affairs with other clubs
- but with Everton it is a marriage!

Everton has been the love of my life for over 30 years, however,
my intimate association with the club could have been very
different. When I was a young player at Preston, I was told that
a Big 5 club had come in for me. I was aware of the rumours and
thought that it must be Liverpool or Tottenham - but it wasn't.
It was Everton and I travelled to Goodison in my red MG to hear
what Harry Catterick had to say. Upon arrival he took one look at my car and declared:
*"Either get it sprayed or prepare for the worst!"* Immediately after signing for Everton
I swapped my pride and joy for a blue model. The club and I have now celebrated our
ruby wedding anniversary - which I suppose is as close an association with the colour
red as you can have as an Evertonian!

Even though I had been the youngest player to appear in an FA Cup final, Harry
Catterick took me to one side and said to me *"Welcome to the big time!"* He was a master
of understatement! Those words rang in my ears as I walked into Bellefield for the first
time and found myself surrounded by super-stars such as Ball, Young, Labone and
Wilson. What also shone through was that each and every one of them genuinely loved
the club. Not surprisingly I also loved my playing days at Everton, the highlight being
the 1969/70 season when we played the best football that I have ever been associated
with and fully lived up to the School of Science mantle.

I must admit, however, that I didn't settle immediately. My debut against Southampton
was a nightmare and, to make matters worse, was one of the few home games that
Everton lost that season. Feeling dejected I drove back to Preston with my father, my
mood was not lifted by the fact that it was pouring with rain. We stopped for petrol
shortly after leaving Goodison and noticed three or four other Evertonians re-fuelling.
I was disappointed by my display and in all honesty preferred not to be recognised.
But one by one these fans knelt down in the puddles in front of my car, raised their arms
and bowed to me. It was an unbelievable sight - one that I can picture vividly to this
day. On that wet Tuesday night - March 18, 1967 - I vowed I would always do my
utmost to please the Everton faithful. I hope that I have lived up to that promise.

Like the majority of former-players, I believe that Everton is a very special club. I made
over 270 appearances and feel honoured to have played alongside some very talented
footballers. With the likes of West, Ball, Harvey and Royle in the side we also developed
a tremendous team spirit, not dissimilar to that nurtured during my first term as manager
some 15 years later when we enjoyed the most successful period in the club's history.
With exceptional players like Southall, Reid, Steven and Sharp in the line-up, we were
voted the 'European Team of 1985'. From my experience in football, which includes
over 500 games in charge of Everton, I am convinced that if English clubs had not
been banned from Europe we would have scaled even greater heights.

Throughout the emotional roller-coaster ride of recent decades I have shared tears of joy
and tears of despair with fellow Evertonians. Perhaps more than anything I have valued
their support. Being denied our place among the elite of Europe, through no fault of
our own, seemed unjust. But there again, nobody said that being an Evertonian would
be easy. Royal blue is not just a flavour of the month - it is a life-long commitment!
I am proud of my blue blood and always will be.

*Howard Kendall*

"So there we were, walking up the steps of the Adelphi and into the cavernous reception area. Blind Date auditions were in the room on the left but no blondes with legs up to their ears could compete with the delights in store. We stood chatting with other Evertonians as player after player joined the throng. Out came Brian, the assistant manager and star of the fly-on-the-wall documentary 'Hotel', to proclaim that the proceedings were to begin. After we had filed into the banqueting hall, compere Mark Owen announced "We know how the music goes!" and to a man everyone began the first stirring notes of 'Z Cars' and it kept going without the tape ever playing. We glanced to the back and through the huge doors came a procession of the greatest Evertonians still alive! Sharpie, Inchy, Ratters, Waggy, Tricky Trev, Stevens, Reid, Lyons, Kendall, Harvey, Hurst, Royle, Kenyon, Wright, Labone, West, Temple, Wilson, Collins, Hickson, Harris, Eglington and others I apologise for forgetting. It was one of those rare shivers down the spine moments.*

*I've been to a few such evenings over the years but nothing compared! The atmosphere was electric - with songs, chants, and good-natured heckling. Above all it was a joy to see the older players, especially Ray Wilson and Tommy Eglington, who stayed long after most of the other players had left, still buzzing, still signing, still having pictures taken and loving every minute of it. The big finish was saved for Howard Kendall, who received the loudest and most overwhelming reception of the evening. As Derek Hatton passionately declared in the middle of the evening "I wish the present players were here to witness the feeling and belief here tonight - so they can realise where they are and what they represent!"*

Mike Royden, *Speke From The Harbour,* April 1999


"If heartfelt aspirations were Premiership points Everton would be so far ahead in the title race that the rest would have given up by now. That much was clear from the intoxicating act of worship that saw 80 Goodison greats being ushered up the royal blue carpet into Gwladys Street's fabled Hall of Fame. Some of those honoured in the fading grandeur of the Adelphi had long departed for the great stadium in the sky. No Billie Dean. No Tommy Lawton. No Joe Mercer. No Roy Vernon. No Harry Catterick. No Peter Farrell. But all were there in spirit on a night when more than 500 Evertonians dined on a meal of Premiership chicken from which the bones had been removed, followed by generous portions of pie in the sky, all washed down with jeroboams of pure adrenaline.

It was a memorable night with due honour being accorded to a pantheon of Goodison gods. Tears were unashamedly shed, firstly by Bill Kenwright who, like Moses, told the faithful to keep taking the tablets. After all, when was medicine anything else but bitter? Apparently there was a happy land, but it was far away. Something like Old Trafford, with a soccer team to match. At that point the crystal ball got so sob-logged it packed up. Reality bit a little, but only when the word 'hamper' was invoked. Otherwise it was a trip to wonderland - a field of blue stretching forever, lined with silver trophies. This was leaving the true world behind. Drugged by past glories, you could believe in miracles. Almost. There was so much happiness around I'm surprised that Peter Johnson didn't break down the door and claim 68 per cent of it. There was so much din, I got away with chanting the name Buckley Finch for later inclusion in what could well be a definitive Hall of Fame. Put my lapse down to export-strength Iron Bru. Put it down to the mind-bending properties of Collins, Kendall, Labone, Royle, Reid, Steven, Ratcliffe and all. Put it down to love and remembrance ... As for the future, well ..."*

Len Capeling, *Liverpool Daily Post,* March 31, 1999

# CONTENTS ...

# FIRST CLUB OF MERSEYSIDE
## Established in 1878

---

### FOOTBALL LEAGUE DIVISION 1
Champions: 1890/91, 1914/15, 1927/28, 1931/32,
1938/39, 1962/63, 1969/70, 1984/85, 1986/87
Runners-up: 1889/90, 1894/95, 1901/02, 1904/05
1908/09, 1911/12, 1985/86

### FOOTBALL LEAGUE DIVISION 2
Champions: 1930/31
Runners-up: 1953/54

### FOOTBALL ASSOCIATION CUP
Winners: 1906, 1933, 1966, 1984, 1995
Runners-up: 1893, 1897, 1968, 1985, 1986, 1989

### FOOTBALL LEAGUE CUP
Runners-up: 1976/77, 1983/84

### EUROPEAN CUP-WINNERS' CUP
Winners: 1984/85

### FOOTBALL ASSOCIATION CHARITY SHIELD
Winners: 1928, 1932, 1963, 1970
1984, 1985, 1987, 1995
Joint Holders: 1986
Runners-up: 1933, 1966

### EMPIRE EXHIBITION CUP
Runners-up: 1938

### SCREEN SPORT SUPER CUP
Runners-up: 1985/86

### SIMOD CUP
Runners-up: 1988/89

### ZENITH DATA SYSTEMS CUP
Runners-up: 1990/91

---

Founder member of the Football League in 1888
Founder member of the FA Premier League in 1992

WALTER ABBOTT · ALAN BALL · BILLY BALMER · JAMES BAXTER · JOHN BELL · BILLY BINGHAM

RICHARD BOYLE · CLIFF BRITTON

## FIRST CLUB OF MERSEYSIDE

BOBBY COLLINS · BILLY COOK · WARNEY CRESSWELL · JIMMY DUNN

TOMMY EGLINGTON · PETER FARRELL · WALLY FIELDING · TOM FLEETWOOD · BERTIE FREEMAN

JIMMY GABRIEL · FRED GEARY · CHARLIE GEE · ALBERT GELDARD · ANDY GRAY · HAROLD HARDMAN

BRIAN HARRIS · HUNTER HART · COLIN HARVEY · ADRIAN HEATH · DAVE HICKSON

JOHNNY HOLT · JOHN HURST · TOMMY JONES · T G JONES · HOWARD KENDALL · ROGER KENYON

BRIAN LABONE · BOB LATCHFORD · ALEX LATTA · TOMMY LAWTON · MIKE LYONS

GEORGE MAHON · HARRY MAKEPEACE · JOE MERCER · ALF MILWARD · JOHN MOORES · JOHNNY MORRISSEY

ALEX PARKER · BOBBY PARKER · JOHN WILLIE PARKER · KEVIN RATCLIFFE · PETER REID

JOE ROYLE · TED SAGAR · BILLY SCOTT · JIMMY SETTLE · GRAEME SHARP

JACK SHARP · KEVIN SHEEDY · NEVILLE SOUTHALL

JACK SOUTHWORTH · JIMMY STEIN · TREVOR STEVEN

ROY VERNON · DAVE WATSON · GORDON WEST

PAUL BRACEWELL · ANDY KING · GORDON WATSON

GWLADYS STREET

The roots of Everton run deep into the bed-rock of Merseyside. Founded in 1878 as St Domingo Football Club, the first club of Merseyside has woven a golden thread through the evolution of the game and its unparalleled heritage has linked generations of proud fans. Thanks in no small way to the opportunism of Graham Stuart, Gareth Farrelly and Kevin Campbell in recent seasons, Everton boast an unrivalled history of 96 seasons in the top flight of English football. Throughout most of this period, blue-blooded patrons have been served fast, flowing football embroidered by the skills of football icons such as Sandy Young, Dixie Dean, Tommy Lawton, Alex Young, Alan Ball and Peter Reid. Gwladys Street's Hall of Fame not only pays homage to these super-stars but also illuminates the exceptional contributions to the royal blue cause made by other great footballers who have not enjoyed the same degree of celebrity.

The Hall of Fame was conceived in 1998 as a celebration of the players and officials who had made significant contributions to the club's welfare. To this end, a panel of former-players, journalists, shareholders and season-ticket holders pains-takingly assessed the playing abilities, club service, team accomplishments and honours earned by candidates during their careers at Everton. No formal guidelines were established, such as prerequisite numbers of first-team appearances or international caps, in order that the panel's appraisals could embrace Everton firsts, records and extra-ordinary feats as well as subjective considerations such as sportsmanship, integrity and popularity with the Goodison faithful. As a result of the original selection exercise in 1998, Hall of Fame membership was extended to five club officials and 75 players representative of all eras.

Of course, it was understood that the compilation of a list of individuals who have done most to enrich royal blue traditions would be a thankless task. Invariably some fans have disagreed with one or two of the original choices and with a few more omissions. Nevertheless, all copies of the earlier editions of this book were quickly snapped-up and no doubt started as many arguments as they resolved. This third edition highlights the Hall of Fame members added in 1999 and profiles the nominees for consideration in 2000, and will doubtless evoke misty-eyed reminiscences of the influential Everton characters of yesteryear who helped establish and reinforce royal blue pride.

HALL OF FAME
STARS

"When I was player-coach at Stoke, Paul Bracewell was one of the boys selected to start the youth programme. He caught the eye of manager Alan Durban and impressed me with his determination to succeed as well as his technical abilities. Although never the quickest of players, Paul learned to do the simple things well and developed a trick or two to get himself out of tight areas. He subsequently played a key role at the heart of Everton's 1984/85 championship team. Sadly he was plagued by an ankle injury picked up at Newcastle in early-1986. Over the next two seasons he showed tremendous courage in overcoming what turned out to be a career-threatening injury."

Howard Kendall

"Refined, cultured, snappy - and that was just his haircut! The floppy fringe which bounced into countless tenacious tackles in 1985 was replaced the following year by a more fitting GI style. The woman responsible for the shaved back and sides was his wife, who also helped me stumble onto an exclusive story three years later. Carol Bracewell worked in a Southport salon and cut my hair. After asking if I wanted shampoo and conditioner, she casually mentioned that Brace was flying to San Francisco for career-saving surgery! The operation was successful - he never did boast a better haircut, though."

David Prentice, *Liverpool Echo*

"When Andy King arrived from Luton, he was a young maverick full of self-confidence and pimples. Despite his teenage complexion, he impressed me with his tremendous technical skills and immense courage. In addition he had a natural eye for goal and scored his fair share. But none was better than his winner against Liverpool in October 1978. His fabulous 20-yard volley broke a seven-year Red jinx. But my celebrations were tinged with the regret that I was reaching the end of my days at Goodison when Andy's flair seemed destined to take Everton to the top."

Roger Kenyon

"It was that goal in 1978 that made him an icon. We had waited seven years for that moment. And it was pure joy and Andy became our king! To me and to all those of a similar age, he was our star man. Martin Dobson looked like your dad, whereas Andy King was your smooth bastard brother. You know, the one that everyone wanted to be like. Andy said that he'd gladly crawl over broken glass to play for Everton. He loved this club of ours and we loved him."

Graham Ennis, *When Skies Are Grey*

"Gordon Watson, my first coach at Everton, had a tremendous influence on me. He was a gentleman from the old school and must have been a fine player to have held his own alongside Mercer and Lawton in the pre-war championship team. Gordon taught me how to pass the ball. Even as a 50-year old he could pass effortlessly with his unbelievably accurate right foot. During my career playing and coaching on both sides of the Atlantic I have marvelled at some of the super-stars of the game but very few could pass the ball like Gordon Watson."

Steve Seargeant, player 1971/71-77/78

"Football mirrors life. Some people hog the limelight whereas others simply work hard at their jobs without receiving the recognition that they deserve. Gordon Watson served Everton for more than 60 years and was an unsung hero for most of them. People tend to forget that he was an important member of arguably the best footballing Everton team of all time and was one of the best passers of the ball in the pre-war game."

TG Jones

Around 750 players have featured in Everton's first-team since the club was established 121 years ago. But in keeping with the club's Latin motto, the likelihood of selection to the Hall of Fame is low and, in fact, the doors of the Hall of Fame were opened to only 10% of these players in 1998. Possibly Gwladys Street's high standards are best reflected in the qualifications of the well-known footballers who have yet to be inducted. In order to correct any oversights and also reflect recent royal blue achievements, it was recognised at the outset that the merits of a handful of candidates would be considered annually. Subscribers to the *Liverpool Daily Post & Echo*, *Speke From The Harbour* fanzine and *Gwladys Street's Hall of Fame* book were invited to participate in the process for electing new members in 1999. Subsequently six nominees were proposed:

☆ Paul Bracewell
☆ Sir Philip Carter
☆ Andy King
☆ Derek Mountfield
☆ Fred Pickering
☆ Gordon Watson

Everton fans taking part in the poll were required to indicate their first and second choices from the short-list of nominees - with first-place votes being awarded two points and second-place votes one point. Approximately 1,400 ballot forms were distributed and some 465 fans voted. The results of the poll are:

|  | first-place votes | second-place votes | % total votes |
|---|---|---|---|
| Bracewell | 119 | 72 | 22.2 % |
| King | 100 | 83 | 20.3 % |
| Watson | 110 | 60 | 20.0 % |
| Mountfield | 66 | 119 | 18.0 % |
| Carter | 57 | 101 | 15.4 % |
| Pickering | 13 | 30 | 4.0 % |

The votes for individual candidates were influenced by the age of the participants. For example the preferred choices of the younger fans were Bracewell and Mountfield, whereas the favourites of older fans were Watson and King.

|  | % votes under 30 years | % votes 30-60 years | % votes over 60 years |
|---|---|---|---|
| Bracewell | 29.0 % | 21.3 % | 11.8 % |
| King | 20.6 % | 20.8 % | 17.6 % |
| Watson | 8.9 % | 18.6 % | 48.5 % |
| Mountfield | 25.2 % | 16.6 % | 8.8 % |
| Carter | 16.3 % | 16.0 % | 11.3 % |
| Pickering | 0.0 % | 6.7 % | 2.0 % |

A panel of respected Evertonians verified the ballot results and concurred that Paul Bracewell, Andy King and Gordon Watson be added to the Hall of Fame in 1999. Surprisingly, none of these players had made 200 League appearances and only Bracewell had earned full-international honours. However, all three were famed for play-making abilities key to the traditions of the School of Science and have demonstrated unwavering commitment to the royal blue cause. Of course, additional members will be added through future ballots. But with free-agents buzzing from club to club, it is anticipated that few players in the post-Bosman era will rub shoulders with Dean, Young, Southall and the other members of the Goodison elite? Very few ever have!

| Caps at Everton | |
|---|---|
| 1 Neville Southall | 92 |
| 2 Kevin Ratcliffe | 58 |
| 3 Kevin Sheedy | 41 |
| 4 Alan Ball | 39 |
| 5 Peter Farrell | 33 |
| 5 Ray Wilson | 33 |
| 7 Tommy Eglington | 28 |
| 8 Brian Labone | 26 |
| 8 Gary Stevens | 26 |
| 10 Trevor Steven | 25 |
| 11 Alex Stevenson | 20 |
| 12 TG Jones | 17 |

| Heavy-Weights | |
|---|---|
| *kg* | |
| 1 Neville Southall | 93.0 |
| 2 TG Jones | 87.2 |
| 3 Gordon West | 86.5 |
| 4 Brian Labone | 86.3 |
| 5 Tommy White | 84.1 |
| 6 Alex Latta | 83.5 |
| 6 Joe Royle | 83.5 |
| 8 Walter Abbott | 83.0 |
| 9 Bob Latchford | 82.5 |
| 10 Jock Thomson | 82.4 |
| 11 Dixie Dean | 82.2 |
| 12 Peter Farrell | 80.8 |

| Marksmen | |
|---|---|
| *goals per game* | |
| 1 Jack Southworth | 1.125 |
| 2 Dixie Dean | 0.885 |
| 3 Fred Geary | 0.878 |
| 4 Bobby Parker | 0.772 |
| 5 Tommy Lawton | 0.737 |
| 6 Bertie Freeman | 0.713 |
| 7 Roy Vernon | 0.555 |
| 8 John Willie Parker | 0.506 |
| 9 Bob Latchford | 0.478 |
| 10 Alex Latta | 0.473 |
| 11 Dave Hickson | 0.457 |
| 12 Joe Royle | 0.431 |

| Big Buys | |
|---|---|
| *£ million* | |
| 1 Dave Watson | 0.900 |
| 2 Adrian Heath | 0.850 |
| 3 Andy King | 0.400 |
| 4 Bob Latchford | 0.350 |
| 5 Trevor Steven | 0.300 |
| 6 Paul Bracewell | 0.350 |
| 6 Andy Gray | 0.250 |
| 8 Neville Southall | 0.150 |
| 9 Graeme Sharp | 0.120 |
| 10 Alan Ball | 0.112 |
| 11 Kevin Sheedy | 0.100 |
| 12 Howard Kendall | 0.080 |

| Living Legends | |
|---|---|
| *year of birth* | |
| 1 Gordon Watson | 1914 |
| 2 TG Jones | 1917 |
| 3 Wally Fielding | 1919 |
| 4 Tommy Eglington | 1923 |
| 5 Dave Hickson | 1929 |
| 6 Tommy Jones | 1930 |
| 7 Bobby Collins | 1931 |
| 8 Billy Bingham | 1931 |
| 9 Ray Wilson | 1934 |
| 10 Brian Harris | 1935 |
| 11 Alex Parker | 1935 |
| 12 Alex Young | 1937 |

| Substitutes | |
|---|---|
| *% total appearances as substitute* | |
| 1 Andy Gray | 11.5% |
| 2 Adrian Heath | 10.4% |
| 3 Roger Kenyon | 6.2% |
| 4 Mike Lyons | 6.0% |
| 5 Graeme Sharp | 4.9% |
| 6 John Hurst | 4.1% |
| 7 Kevin Sheedy | 3.6% |
| 8 Peter Reid | 2.6% |
| 9 Ray Wilson | 2.0% |
| 10 Andy King | 1.7% |
| 11 Paul Bracewell | 1.6% |
| 12 Trevor Steven | 1.4% |

The members of Gwladys Street's Hall of Fame are presented alphabetically, not as a league table but as a directory of the significant contributors to the development of the club. Their brief profiles are intended to highlight their backgrounds, characteristics, accomplishments and playing records at Everton. Because this publication was written by an Evertonian for fellow Evertonians, these profiles may be considered prone to hyperbole by those of other persuasions.

Players' records can be a minefield of errors. The reported data are limited to appearances and goals in the Football League and Premier League, FA Challenge Cup (also the English Cup), European and other major competitions. The latter category includes the FA Full Members' Cup (also the Simod Cup and Zenith Data Systems Cup), FA Charity Shield, Football League Cup (also the Milk Cup, Rumbelows League Cup, Littlewoods Challenge Cup, Coca-Cola Cup and Worthington Cup), Football League Centenary, Texaco Challenge Cup, British Championship Decider, Empire Exhibition Cup and Screen Sport Super Cup and excludes friendlies, testimonial games and regional competitions.

# WALTER ABBOTT

*Walter Abbott matured into a powerhouse player with a game based on honest graft.*

After cutting his teeth with Rosewood Victoria, Abbott joined Everton from Small Heath (Birmingham City) for £250. The 21-year old packed a stunning shot and had scored 36 goals as an inside-forward with the Midlands-outfit during the 1898/99 season. However, his goal-scoring prowess initially deserted him at Everton and he was converted into a tough-tackling left-half.

At 83.0 kg, Abbott liked to throw his weight around and was the most intimidating player in the Everton sides around the turn of the century. He was very difficult to dispossess and developed a reputation for never shirking a tackle as he covered every inch of the pitch. Abbott matured into a key member of two English Cup final teams and collected a winners' medal for the 1906 triumph over Newcastle United.

Surprisingly, Abbott gained only modest international recognition. He appeared for the Football League against the Irish League in 1901 and was awarded his solitary England cap against Wales in 1902, at centre-half - a position he had never played for Everton in Division 1. Abbott moved to Burnley in 1908 before closing out his career with Birmingham.

Born: Small Heath, Birmingham, 1877
Height: 1.80 m (5 ft 11 in) Weight: 83.0 kg (13 st 1 lb)

|  | League apps | League goals | FA Cup apps | FA Cup goals | Total apps | Total goals |
|---|---|---|---|---|---|---|
| 1899/00 | 25 | 1 | 1 | 0 | 26 | 1 |
| 1900/01 | 34 | 5 | 2 | 0 | 36 | 5 |
| 1901/02 | 31 | 4 | 2 | 0 | 33 | 4 |
| 1902/03 | 33 | 4 | 3 | 2 | 36 | 6 |
| 1903/04 | 32 | 4 | 1 | 0 | 33 | 4 |
| 1904/05 | 28 | 4 | 6 | 0 | 34 | 4 |
| 1905/06 | 27 | 5 | 5 | 1 | 32 | 6 |
| 1906/07 | 26 | 4 | 7 | 1 | 33 | 5 |
| 1907/08 | 21 | 1 | 7 | 1 | 28 | 2 |
|  | 257 | 32 | 34 | 5 | 291 | 37 |

**Honours at Everton**
FA Cup (English Cup) winner: 1906
FA Cup (English Cup) runner-up: 1907
Division 1 runner-up: 1901/02, 1904/05
Caps for England: 1
Appearances for the Football League: 3

# ALAN BALL

*Alan Ball was the best mid-fielder of his era,*
*arguably the hardest working of all-time.*

Ball was turned down by Wolverhampton Wanderers and spurned by Bolton Wanderers before signing for Blackpool. He matured quickly at Bloomfield Road and as a 21-year old joined the elite band of players to have won a World Cup winners' medal. The England star moved to Everton for a British record fee of £112,000 in 1966.

Ball combined brilliant ball skills, including a superb first touch, with indefatigable stamina. At Everton, he blossomed into a charismatic crowd-pleaser and an explosive match-winner capable of contributing 20 goals per season. Alongside the significant talents of Howard Kendall and Colin Harvey, Ball consistently served up enterprising displays of rich and flowing football. The mid-field triumvirate worked flat out, scampering up and down the pitch for the full 90 minutes of every game and dominated Division 1 throughout the 1969/70 championship campaign. But astonishingly, the Goodison idol was sold to Arsenal for £220,000 in 1971. Everton's directors claimed satisfaction with doubling their money after five years of superior service.

Before hanging up his famous white boots, Ball continued his nomadic playing career with Southampton, Blackpool and Bristol Rovers and journeyed farther afield for stints at Vancouver Whitecaps (Canada) and Bulova (Hong Kong). He moved into football management during his second spell at Blackpool and also served Portsmouth, Stoke City, Colchester United, Exeter City, Southampton and Manchester City. He returned to Portsmouth in 1998.

Ball was a truly world-class footballer and an unshakeable mainstay in the England international set-up for more than a decade. He earned 39 of his total 72 caps during his all-too-short stay at Goodison Park.

Born: Farnworth, 1945
Height: 1.68 m (5 ft 6 in)   Weight: 64.0 kg (10 st 1 lb)

| | League apps | goals | FA Cup apps | goals | Other apps | goals | Europe apps | goals | Total apps | goals |
|---|---|---|---|---|---|---|---|---|---|---|
| 1966/67 | 41 | 15 | 6 | 2 | 0 | 0 | 4 | 1 | 51 | 18 |
| 1967/68 | 34 | 20 | 4 | 0 | 2 | 0 | 0 | 0 | 40 | 20 |
| 1968/69 | 40 | 16 | 5 | 0 | 4 | 2 | 0 | 0 | 49 | 18 |
| 1969/70 | 37 | 10 | 1 | 1 | 3 | 1 | 0 | 0 | 41 | 12 |
| 1970/71 | 39 | 2 | 5 | 2 | 1 | 0 | 6 | 3 | 51 | 7 |
| 1971/72 | 17 | 3 | 0 | 0 | 1 | 0 | 0 | 0 | 18 | 3 |
| | 208 | 66 | 21 | 5 | 11 | 3 | 10 | 4 | 250 | 78 |

**Honours at Everton**
Division 1 winner: 1969/70
FA Cup runner-up: 1968
Caps for England: 39
Appearances for the Football League: 3

# BILLY BALMER

*Billy Balmer confounded his critics*
*by emerging as a formidable full-back.*

The West Derby native joined Everton as a 20-year old from South Shore (Blackpool) in 1897 and established a famous partnership with Irish international Jack Crelley. The sturdy defender was equally as comfortable on either flank and towards the end of his Goodison career developed a similarly effective understanding with his younger brother, Robert Balmer.

Although the full-back's game was not without flaws, he was quick and possessed the other major prerequisites of a reliable defender at the turn of the century - powerful shoulder charges, crunching tackles and hefty clearances. Given these attributes, Balmer was considered a sure-footed and occasionally dashing performer during a period in which the Toffees came tantalisingly close to capturing the Division 1 crown. Staunch defending enabled Everton to finish in the top three on four occasions between 1901/02-1906/07.

In addition, Balmer featured in two consecutive cup finals with Everton and was one of the lesser known members of the 1906 team which brought the English Cup to Merseyside for the first time. He represented the Football League against the Scottish League in 1901 and was also capped by England against Ireland in 1905. Balmer moved to Croydon Common of the Southern League in 1908. He later became a trainer at Huddersfield Town.

Born: Liverpool, 1877
Height: 1.73 m (5 ft 8 in)  Weight: 73.1 kg (11 st 7 lb)

|         | League apps | League goals | FA Cup apps | FA Cup goals | Total apps | Total goals |
|---------|-------------|--------------|-------------|--------------|------------|-------------|
| 1897/98 | 12          | 0            | 5           | 0            | 17         | 0           |
| 1898/99 | 23          | 0            | 2           | 0            | 25         | 0           |
| 1899/00 | 32          | 1            | 1           | 0            | 33         | 1           |
| 1900/01 | 31          | 0            | 2           | 0            | 33         | 0           |
| 1901/02 | 28          | 0            | 2           | 0            | 30         | 0           |
| 1902/03 | 28          | 0            | 3           | 0            | 31         | 0           |
| 1903/04 | 32          | 0            | 1           | 0            | 33         | 0           |
| 1904/05 | 30          | 0            | 3           | 0            | 33         | 0           |
| 1905/06 | 18          | 0            | 5           | 0            | 23         | 0           |
| 1906/07 | 33          | 0            | 8           | 0            | 41         | 0           |
| 1907/08 | 26          | 0            | 6           | 0            | 32         | 0           |
|         | 293         | 1            | 38          | 0            | 331        | 1           |

### Honours at Everton
FA Cup (English Cup) winner: 1906
FA Cup (English Cup) runner-up: 1907
Division 1 runner-up: 1901/02, 1904/05
Caps for England: 1
Appearances for the Football League: 1

# DR JAMES BAXTER

*James Clement Baxter was Everton's first major benefactor.*

Baxter, along with many club members, was unhappy with the state of affairs at Anfield Road and supported George Mahon in leading the 1892 exodus from the ground and the Sandon Hotel headquarters. To fund the ambitious re-location to Mere Green Field, Everton formed a limited liability company with 2,500 ordinary shares at £1 each and 100 mortgage debenture bonds at £10 each. Baxter augmented these funds by advancing an unsecured, interest-free loan of £1,000 to the new company. His generosity allowed Everton to expedite the levelling of the neglected nursery land and the erection of a grandstand and two uncovered enclosures for the start of the 1892/93 season.

Educated at St Francis Xavier's College and based at his Robson Street surgery, Baxter was respected by the mostly Irish immigrants in his Everton district as a genuine man of the people. He represented the Liberal Party on Liverpool City Council between 1906-1920 and showed particular interest in transportation and electric power issues. At one time he worked with JA Brodie, the city engineer and inventor of goal nets. The local physician was also devoted to the welfare of Everton and was elected to the club's committee in 1889. Conspicuous for his tact as for his tireless energy, he served as a director for 35 years and enjoyed several terms as club chairman. Also in the early days, he doubled as the club's medical adviser.

Everton made tremendous strides under the stewardship of Baxter and Mahon. They constructed one of the first purpose-built football stadiums in Europe, attracted quality professional footballers from around the country and earned a world-wide reputation for cultured play. In addition, the club captured the League championship and the English Cup and was unfortunate not to win both trophies on several other occasions around the turn of the century.

Baxter also found time to work on the Football League Management Committee for 15 years and the Football Association Council for four years. Upon his death in 1928, he was succeeded as an Everton director by his son - Dr Cecil Baxter.

Born: Liverpool, 1857
**Everton director/chairman:** 35 years

**Everton record during term**
League: 576 wins, 275 draws, 449 defeats

**Everton honours during term**
League champions: 1890/91
Division 1 champions: 1914/15
League runners-up: 1889/90
Division 1 runners-up: 1894/95, 1901/02, 1904/05, 1908/09, 1911/12
FA Cup (English Cup) winners: 1906
FA Cup (English Cup) runners-up: 1893, 1897, 1907

# JOHN BELL

*John Bell was a talented footballer
who demonstrated flair for the unusual.*

Previously with Dumbarton Union and Dumbarton, the skillful and inventive winger had been labelled the wonder-kid of Dumbarton's Scottish League championship team of 1891/92. Bell arrived at Everton in the aftermath of the 1893 English Cup final loss to Wolverhampton Wanderers and soon gained the affection and esteem of his team-mates and fans. As a gifted entertainer, he enthralled the congregation at newly-opened Goodison Park with his breath-taking ball skills and his unpredictable and irascible abilities to produce something out of nothing.

Something of a heavyweight at 80.0 kg, Bell was renowned for his speed off the mark, deft touches and bewildering chicanery. Equally as dangerous on either wing, the master dribbler played as though the ball was tied to his boot laces. But after making 147 appearances for the club and starring in the 1897 English Cup final, he left Everton to play for New Brighton Tower and Celtic, where he earned Scottish Cup winners' medals in 1899 and 1900. Surprisingly, he returned to Everton in 1901 and made another 52 appearances for the Toffees before joining Preston North End as player-coach. He steered the Lancashire-club to the Division 2 title in 1904.

Bell earned three of his 10 Scotland caps during his time at Goodison and was so well-respected by his peers that they elected him chairman of the first player's union. But perhaps he will be best remembered on Merseyside for scoring the first-ever goal in a League derby game, when Everton defeated Liverpool by 3-0 in front of a vociferous crowd of 44,000 in 1894.

Born: Dumbarton, 1870
Height: 1.80 m (5 ft 11 in)  Weight: 80.0 kg (12 st 8 lb)

|  | League apps | League goals | FA Cup apps | FA Cup goals | Total apps | Total goals |
|---|---|---|---|---|---|---|
| 1892/93 | 3 | 0 | 0 | 0 | 3 | 0 |
| 1893/94 | 24 | 9 | 1 | 0 | 25 | 9 |
| 1894/95 | 27 | 15 | 3 | 3 | 30 | 18 |
| 1895/96 | 27 | 9 | 3 | 1 | 30 | 10 |
| 1896/97 | 27 | 15 | 5 | 2 | 32 | 17 |
| 1897/98 | 22 | 4 | 5 | 0 | 27 | 4 |
| 1901/02 | 24 | 5 | 2 | 0 | 26 | 5 |
| 1902/03 | 23 | 5 | 3 | 2 | 26 | 7 |
|  | 177 | 62 | 22 | 8 | 199 | 70 |

**Honours at Everton**
FA Cup (English Cup) runner-up: 1897
Division 1 runner-up: 1894/95, 1901/02
Caps for Scotland: 3

# BILLY BINGHAM

*Billy Bingham enjoyed playing success
but later endured management frustrations.*

The veteran winger had enjoyed spells with Glentoran, Sunderland and Luton Town before transferring to Everton in 1960. The transaction involved John Bramwell, Alec Ashworth and £15,000 moving to Kenilworth Road in exchange for the established Northern Ireland star.

Bingham had reinforced his international reputation for outwitting and outstripping defences during the 1958 World Cup in Sweden. At Goodison Park, he joined a star-studded team bristling with attacking flair and displayed his sublime dribbling skills as well as his unerring eye for goal. The right-winger contributed towards the Toffees capturing the Division 1 championship in 1962/63. But with his first-team place threatened by the arrival of Alex Scott, Bingham moved to Port Vale in 1963.

The Ulsterman's management career took in Southport, Linfield and Plymouth Argyle as well as the national sides of Northern Ireland and Greece before he accepted the Goodison post in 1973. Bingham inherited an Everton playing staff in need of rejuvenation and is remembered for selling Kendall, Harvey and Royle as much as for purchasing Latchford, Rioch and McKenzie. His team came close to realising its potential in 1974/75, when Everton led the Division 1 race for most of the season. However, they faltered by taking only seven points from their final 10 games and faded to fourth position.

Bingham, who had gained a dozen of his 56 international caps with Everton, left the club in 1977 to take charge of PAOK Salonika (Greece), Mansfield Town and subsequently the Northern Ireland national side. Under his leadership, Northern Ireland qualified for the World Cup finals in Spain in 1982 and Mexico in 1986. He was awarded the MBE for services to football.

Born: Belfast, 1931
Height: 1.69 m (5 ft 7 in)  Weight: 72.6 kg (11 st 6 lb)

|  | League apps | League goals | FA Cup apps | FA Cup goals | Other apps | Other goals | Europe apps | Europe goals | Total apps | Total goals |
|---|---|---|---|---|---|---|---|---|---|---|
| 1960/61 | 26 | 9 | 1 | 0 | 3 | 1 | 0 | 0 | 30 | 10 |
| 1961/62 | 37 | 9 | 3 | 1 | 0 | 0 | 0 | 0 | 40 | 10 |
| 1962/63 | 23 | 5 | 3 | 1 | 0 | 0 | 2 | 0 | 28 | 6 |
|  | 86 | 23 | 7 | 2 | 3 | 1 | 2 | 0 | 98 | 26 |

**Honours at Everton**
Division 1 winner: 1962/63
Caps for Northern Ireland: 12

**Management record at Everton 1972/73-1976/77**
League: 53 wins, 48 draws, 45 defeats

# RICHARD BOYLE

*Dickie Boyle never received the honours
that his talents merited.*

Boyle was attracted to the golden carrot of English football in 1892 and arrived on
Merseyside after fleeting stays at Dumbarton Episcopalians, Dumbarton Union and
Dumbarton. Within months of him signing for Everton, the club relocated from Walton
Breck Road, Anfield to pastures new. The young half-back found Goodison Park to be
the ideal stage for displaying his significant talents.

Boyle was an enthusiastic motivator of his new team-mates and quickly assumed the
club captaincy, an important role in the pioneering days of Victorian football. Although
physically small, he was a strong and hustling right-half renowned as much for his
bone-crunching tackles as his incisive passes. His defensive qualities also made
him a natural deputy for Johnny Holt at centre-half.

Unfortunately the major honours of the game eluded him. Boyle captained the Toffees in
two English Cup finals but was on the losing sides on both occasions. To compound his
disappointments, Everton also finished runners-up in the League title race in 1894/95.
Boyle remained on the brink of international honours but was never capped by Scotland.
He eventually forfeited his first-team place to Tommy Booth and played only a couple
of games for Everton after the turn of the century before winding down his
career with Dundee.

Born: Dumbarton, circa 1870
Height: 1.65 m (5 ft 5 in)  Weight: 66.5 kg (10 st 6 in)

|  | League apps | League goals | FA Cup apps | FA Cup goals | Total apps | Total goals |
|---|---|---|---|---|---|---|
| 1892/93 | 25 | 0 | 7 | 0 | 32 | 0 |
| 1893/94 | 21 | 1 | 0 | 0 | 21 | 1 |
| 1894/95 | 30 | 2 | 4 | 0 | 34 | 2 |
| 1895/96 | 30 | 3 | 3 | 0 | 33 | 3 |
| 1896/97 | 29 | 0 | 5 | 1 | 34 | 1 |
| 1897/98 | 22 | 0 | 0 | 0 | 22 | 0 |
| 1898/99 | 34 | 1 | 2 | 0 | 36 | 1 |
| 1899/00 | 29 | 0 | 0 | 0 | 29 | 0 |
| 1900/01 | 2 | 0 | 0 | 0 | 2 | 0 |
|  | 222 | 7 | 21 | 1 | 243 | 8 |

**Honours at Everton**
FA Cup (English Cup) runner-up: 1893, 1897
Division 1 runner-up: 1894/95

# PAUL BRACEWELL

*Paul Bracewell contributed to the halcyon days of the 1984/85 campaign.*

The Heswall native was groomed by Stoke City and signed by manager Howard Kendall from Sunderland for £250,000 in 1984. Bracewell was the ideal complement to Peter Reid at the centre of the Everton engine room and his ball-winning tackles, precise passes and inexhaustible stamina contributed towards the club's domestic and European successes during the 1984/85 campaign. He was rewarded with his first England international cap in 1985, as substitute against West Germany.

Unfortunately Bracewell's career was dogged by a serious ankle injury sustained at Newcastle United in early-1986. He played out the remainder of the campaign, often in agony, as Everton chased a League-cup double. Subsequently, Bracewell underwent a series of operations and did not feature in the Everton line-up for two seasons. By that time Howard Kendall had moved to Spain and the sun was setting on the Goodison glory years. Nevertheless, he contributed to the 1989 FA Cup run and, in fact, made his final appearance for Everton at Wembley. Bracewell and Gary Lineker hold the distinction of being the only Everton players to have pulled on the famous royal blue shirt for both the first and the last time at Wembley.

Bracewell returned to Sunderland for £250,000 at the end of the 1988/89 season and, after leaving Goodison, notched up over 300 appearances with Sunderland, Newcastle United and Fulham. He was appointed manager at Craven Cottage in 1999.

Born: Heswall, 1962
Height: 1.72 m (5 ft 8 in) Weight: 68.1 kg (10 st 10 lb)

|  | League apps | goals | FA Cup apps | goals | Other apps | goals | Europe apps | goals | Total apps | goals |
|---|---|---|---|---|---|---|---|---|---|---|
| 1984/85 | 32 | 2 | 7 | 0 | 5 | 1 | 8 | 1 | 52 | 4 |
| 1985/86 | 38 | 3 | 6 | 0 | 10 | 1 | 0 | 0 | 54 | 4 |
| 1986/87 | 0 | 0 | 0 | 0 | 0 | 0 | 0 | 0 | 0 | 0 |
| 1987/88 | 0 | 0 | 0/2 | 0 | 4/1 | 0 | 0 | 0 | 4/3 | 0 |
| 1988/89 | 20 | 2 | 6 | 0 | 1 | 0 | 0 | 0 | 27 | 2 |
|  | 92 | 7 | 19/2 | 0 | 20/1 | 2 | 8 | 1 | 137/3 | 10 |

**Honours at Everton**
Division 1 winner: 1984/85
Division 1 runner-up: 1985/86
European Cup-Winners' Cup winner: 1985
FA Cup runner-up: 1985, 1986, 1989
Caps for England: 3
Caps for England Under-21: 1

# CLIFF BRITTON

*Cliff Britton was one of the most stylish players to have represented Everton and England.*

Bought from Bristol Rovers in 1930, Britton matured into an intelligent wing-half and justified his £2,500 transfer fee by establishing productive partnerships with Jock Thomson and Joe Mercer. Britton excelled at everything that he did. The virtuoso footballer was one of the first ball-playing wing-halves and a founder of Goodison's School of Science. His text-book technique blossomed alongside Mercer and the Everton pair teamed up with Stan Cullis of Wolverhampton Wanderers to form a formidable international half-back line for England. First capped against Wales in 1934, Britton represented his country on nine occasions and also participated in 12 war-time internationals. He also earned an FA Cup winners' medal in 1933 but missed out on the club's championship triumphs in 1931/32 and 1938/39.

After retiring from playing, Britton gained management experience with Burnley prior to his appointment as general manager at Goodison Park in 1948. Sadly, the great expectations that had preceded him went unfulfilled and Everton were relegated to Division 2 at the end of the disastrous 1950/51 campaign for the second time in their illustrious history. Under Britton's stewardship, the club focused on youth development initiatives rather than investing in the transfer market. As a result, the inexperienced Toffees plummeted to sixteenth position before coming to terms with life in Division 2. After three miserable seasons, Britton steered Everton back to the big-time. He left the club at the end of the 1955/56 season and was replaced by Ian Buchan. Britton subsequently managed Preston North End and Hull City.

Born: Hanham, Bristol, 1909
Height: 1.78 m (5 ft 10 in) Weight: 70.0 kg (11 st 0 lb)

|  | League apps | League goals | FA Cup apps | FA Cup goals | Other apps | Other goals | Total apps | Total goals |
|---|---|---|---|---|---|---|---|---|
| 1930/31 | 10 | 0 | 0 | 0 | 0 | 0 | 10 | 0 |
| 1932/33 | 36 | 0 | 6 | 0 | 1 | 0 | 43 | 0 |
| 1933/34 | 42 | 0 | 1 | 0 | 1 | 0 | 44 | 0 |
| 1934/35 | 36 | 0 | 5 | 0 | 0 | 0 | 41 | 0 |
| 1935/36 | 25 | 2 | 1 | 0 | 0 | 0 | 26 | 2 |
| 1936/37 | 40 | 0 | 4 | 1 | 0 | 0 | 44 | 1 |
| 1937/38 | 31 | 0 | 2 | 0 | 0 | 0 | 33 | 0 |
| 1938/39 | 1 | 0 | 0 | 0 | 0 | 0 | 1 | 0 |
|  | 221 | 2 | 19 | 1 | 2 | 0 | 242 | 3 |

### Honours at Everton
FA Cup winner: 1933
Caps for England: 9
War-time internationals: 12
Appearances for the Football League: 4

### Management record at Everton 1948/49-1955/56
League: 115 wins, 93 draws, 128 defeats
Division 2 runners-up: 1953/54

# MR HARRY CATTERICK

*Harry Catterick was an astute manager who
assembled two championship-winning teams.*

Catterick was plucked from the obscurity of Cheadle Heath Nomads. Although he was unable to fill Tommy Lawton's football boots, the bustling centre-forward notched 24 goals in 71 post-war games with Everton before moving to Crewe Alexandra. After gaining management experience with Rochdale and Sheffield Wednesday, Catterick accepted the Everton hot-seat in 1961. He savoured tremendous success and his accomplishments compared favourably with those of Busby, Nicholson, Revie and Shankly. Under his management, the Toffees finished outside the top six on only one occasion and that was in 1966 when they captured the FA Cup.

Renowned as a strict disciplinarian and a tough taskmaster, Catterick inherited a galaxy of expensive signings and transformed them into Division 1 champions within two years. The Everton manager confirmed that money could buy success. Aided by John Moores' cheque book, Catterick wheeled and dealt in the transfer market to strengthen his playing staff by diligently targeting the international stars on his wish-list. After his plans were disrupted when Tony Kay was jailed after the football bribes trial in 1965, Catterick concentrated on grooming home-grown talents and successfully nurtured one of the most entertaining football teams of all time.

Driven by Kendall, Harvey & Ball, Catterick's School of Science raced away with the 1969/70 title towards the threshold of invincibility. Then inexplicably, performances deteriorated and the young team was broken up. Catterick struggled to re-discover his alchemy and, after suffering a period of ill-health, moved into a senior executive position at the club. He later spent two seasons in charge of Preston North End. Catterick died at Goodison Park in 1985.

Born: Darlington, 1919
Height: 1.78 m (5 ft 10 in) Weight: 74.5 kg (11 st 10 lb)

|  | League | | FA Cup | | Total | |
|---|---|---|---|---|---|---|
|  | apps | goals | apps | goals | apps | goals |
| 1945/46 | 0 | 0 | 2 | 1 | 2 | 1 |
| 1946/47 | 3 | 0 | 0 | 0 | 3 | 0 |
| 1947/48 | 9 | 2 | 4 | 1 | 13 | 3 |
| 1948/49 | 10 | 3 | 1 | 0 | 11 | 3 |
| 1949/50 | 20 | 9 | 5 | 3 | 25 | 12 |
| 1950/51 | 13 | 5 | 0 | 0 | 13 | 5 |
| 1951/52 | 4 | 0 | 0 | 0 | 4 | 0 |
|  | 59 | 19 | 12 | 5 | 71 | 24 |

**Management record at Everton 1961/62-1972/73**
League: 224 wins, 139 draws, 141 defeats
Division 1 champions: 1962/63, 1969/70
FA Cup winners: 1966
FA Cup runners-up: 1968

# EDGAR CHADWICK

*Edgar Chadwick was one of the household names of Victorian football.*

Chadwick had starred with Blackburn Olympic and Blackburn Rovers before joining Everton in 1888. He made an immediate impact at Anfield and was the club's leading scorer and only ever-present during the inaugural season of the Football League. Although several clubs had considered Chadwick too frail for the rigours of professional football, he confounded his critics by developing into a resourceful inside-forward. He made 300 first-team appearances during his 11 seasons with Everton and his left-wing partnership with Alf Milward was regarded as the best in the land.

Chadwick helped the Toffees clinch the League championship in 1890/91 but experienced more than his fair share of near-misses. He appeared in three FA Cup finals during his career but was on the losing sides in 1893 and 1897 with Everton and in 1902 with Southampton. Also, he was a member of the Everton teams which narrowly failed to capture the League title on several occasions, finishing runners-up in 1889/90 and 1894/95. Notwithstanding, his talents were rewarded with seven England caps. Coincidentally, five of these earned were against Scotland. Chadwick is remembered north of the border for silencing Ibrox Park in 1892, when he grabbed a sensational goal after only 10 seconds - without a Scottish opponent touching the ball. He also participated in the inaugural inter-League match played that year. The pioneering professional left Goodison for Burnley in 1899 and later turned out for Southampton, Liverpool, Blackpool, Glossop and Darwen.

Born: Blackburn, 1869
Height: 1.65 m (5 ft 5 in)   Weight: 63.5 kg (10 st 0 lb)

|  | League apps | League goals | FA Cup apps | FA Cup goals | Total apps | Total goals |
|---|---|---|---|---|---|---|
| 1888/89 | 22 | 6 | 0 | 0 | 22 | 6 |
| 1889/90 | 22 | 9 | 2 | 0 | 24 | 9 |
| 1890/91 | 22 | 10 | 1 | 0 | 23 | 10 |
| 1891/92 | 25 | 10 | 1 | 1 | 26 | 11 |
| 1892/93 | 27 | 10 | 7 | 7 | 34 | 13 |
| 1893/94 | 24 | 13 | 0 | 0 | 24 | 13 |
| 1894/95 | 28 | 11 | 4 | 3 | 32 | 14 |
| 1895/96 | 28 | 11 | 3 | 1 | 31 | 12 |
| 1896/97 | 28 | 7 | 5 | 2 | 33 | 9 |
| 1897/98 | 22 | 8 | 5 | 2 | 27 | 10 |
| 1898/99 | 22 | 2 | 2 | 1 | 24 | 3 |
| | 270 | 97 | 30 | 13 | 300 | 110 |

**Honours at Everton**
League winner: 1890/91
League runner-up: 1889/90
Division 1 runner-up: 1894/95
FA Cup (English Cup) runner-up: 1893, 1897
Caps for England: 7
Appearances for the Football League: 3

# SAM CHEDGZOY

*Sam Chedgzoy's initiative brought about*
*a change in the laws of the game.*

Chedgzoy exploited a loophole in the rule-book during a game at White Hart Lane in 1924. He took a corner by dribbling along the by-line and hammering the ball into Tottenham's net. Although the goal was disallowed, the football authorities decided after the game that his approach had been legal. The exercise was reported to have been instigated by Ernest Edwards, a Merseyside journalist, and to prevent similar initiatives the 'Chedgzoy Rule' was introduced whereby the taker of a corner kick may only play the ball once.

The innovative outside-right was recruited as a 20-year old from Burnell's Iron Works of the West Cheshire League. He had been spotted by former-Everton star Fred Geary. Chedgzoy was noted for his blistering pace, bewitching close technique and hanging centres and used these significant attributes to lay on many goal-scoring opportunities for centre-forward Bobby Parker during the 1914/15 campaign. Not surprisingly, their combined efforts resulted in the Toffees capturing their second League title.

His accomplishments were severely interrupted by World War I. Nevertheless, he developed into the most inventive football talent to have emerged for decades and enjoyed an illustrious career at Goodison which spanned over 15 years. Chedgzoy received eight England caps, the first against Wales in 1920 when a 30-year old veteran, and also represented the Football League on five occasions, playing against the Scottish League both before and after the hostilities. He finally hung up his boots at the age of 36 and emigrated to North America.

Born: Ellesmere Port, 1890
Height: 1.73 m (5 ft 8 in) Weight: 72.6 kg (11 st 6 lb)

| | League apps | goals | FA Cup apps | goals | Total apps | goals |
|---|---|---|---|---|---|---|
| 1910/11 | 3 | 0 | 0 | 0 | 3 | 0 |
| 1912/13 | 1 | 0 | 0 | 0 | 1 | 0 |
| 1913/14 | 7 | 1 | 0 | 0 | 7 | 1 |
| 1914/15 | 30 | 2 | 5 | 1 | 35 | 3 |
| 1919/20 | 18 | 3 | 1 | 0 | 19 | 3 |
| 1920/21 | 35 | 5 | 5 | 0 | 40 | 5 |
| 1921/22 | 35 | 5 | 1 | 0 | 36 | 5 |
| 1922/23 | 36 | 3 | 2 | 1 | 38 | 4 |
| 1923/24 | 38 | 5 | 2 | 1 | 40 | 6 |
| 1924/25 | 38 | 2 | 3 | 0 | 41 | 2 |
| 1925/26 | 38 | 7 | 2 | 0 | 40 | 7 |
| | 279 | 33 | 21 | 3 | 300 | 36 |

**Honours at Everton**
Division 1 winner: 1914/15
Caps for England: 8
Appearances for the Football League: 5

# BOBBY COLLINS

*Bobby Collins was one of the finest players to have worn the blues of Everton and Scotland.*

Collins almost joined Everton as a junior in 1948 but failed to settle and returned to Glasgow homesick. At 1.62 m, the little inside-forward seemed ill-equipped for the professional fray. But as it turned out, he became one of the post-war stars of the Scottish League. Collins had the lot and was renowned for his exquisite passing, fierce tackling and insatiable appetite for work.

He was signed from Celtic in 1958 for a club record fee of £23,550 and within weeks had become the heart-beat of Everton. The 'Mighty Atom' of the Scottish League returned to Goodison at a time when the Toffees were struggling to retain their Division 1 status. In fact, he was signed by chairman Dick Searle because the club was between managers.

Immediately, Collins rolled up his sleeves and inspired major improvements in results to lead the Toffees out of the relegation mire. Although the Scotland star collected few honours during his four royal blue seasons, he was admired by his team-mates and worshiped by the Goodison faithful. Collins made legions of friends and was re-christened the 'Little General' of Merseyside football.

Collins gained six caps during his invigorating spell at Everton but, shortly after the arrival of new manager Harry Catterick, was sold to Leeds United for £30,000 in 1962. Predictably, he steered the Yorkshire-club back into the first division and was recalled to the Scotland team. Collins was elected PFA 'Footballer of the Year' in 1965. Subsequently, the pocket dynamo served Bury, Morton, Ringwood City (Australia), Hakoah (Australia) and Oldham Athletic. He later experienced the frustrations of football management with Huddersfield Town, Hull City and Barnsley.

Born: Glasgow, 1931
Height: 1.62 m (5 ft 4 in) Weight: 64.9 kg (10 st 3 lb)

| | League apps | goals | FA Cup apps | goals | Other apps | goals | Total apps | goals |
|---|---|---|---|---|---|---|---|---|
| 1958/59 | 32 | 7 | 4 | 3 | 0 | 0 | 36 | 10 |
| 1959/60 | 42 | 14 | 1 | 0 | 0 | 0 | 43 | 14 |
| 1960/61 | 40 | 16 | 1 | 0 | 5 | 1 | 46 | 17 |
| 1961/62 | 19 | 5 | 3 | 2 | 0 | 0 | 22 | 7 |
| | 133 | 42 | 9 | 5 | 5 | 1 | 147 | 48 |

**Honours at Everton**
Caps for Scotland: 6

# BILLY COOK

*Tough tackling Billy Cook was an Irishman
who tasted success in Scotland and England.*

Signed from Celtic for £3,000 in 1932, the no-nonsense defender had collected several honours during his stint in green and white hoops. He had won a Scottish Cup winners' medal in 1931 as well as four Northern Ireland caps.

Cook was a brave and uncompromising defender who was equally at home at right-back or left-back. He applied his football skills with combative ambition and policed the opposition with a fine turn of speed, a ferocious tackle and the ability to knock an opponent off the ball. Unquestionably Cook was one of the most determined full-backs of his generation. He established a formidable rearguard partnership with the more graceful Warney Cresswell and football's beauty and beast were firm favourites at Goodison Park for four seasons.

Cook enjoyed a rewarding spell on Merseyside and was a regular member of the Everton teams which won the FA Cup in 1933 and the Division 1 title in the 1938/39 season. Also he was selected to represent his country on 12 occasions during his time with Everton, his last international outing being against Wales in 1939.

At the conclusion of World War II, the Northern Ireland star was transferred to Wrexham and later became player-manager at Rhyl. He later strayed farther afield to coach Sunderland, Portadown, SK Brann (Norway) and the national teams of Peru and Iraq. Cook also managed Wigan Athletic and Crewe Alexandra before joining the training staff at Norwich City in 1958.

Born: Coleraine, 1909
Height: 1.73 m (5 ft 8 in)  Weight: 77.2 kg (12 st 2 lb)

| | League | | FA Cup | | Other | | Total | |
|---|---|---|---|---|---|---|---|---|
| | apps | goals | apps | goals | apps | goals | apps | goals |
| 1932/33 | 20 | 0 | 6 | 0 | 0 | 0 | 26 | 0 |
| 1933/34 | 35 | 0 | 1 | 0 | 0 | 0 | 36 | 0 |
| 1934/35 | 29 | 0 | 5 | 0 | 1 | 0 | 35 | 0 |
| 1935/36 | 25 | 0 | 1 | 0 | 0 | 0 | 26 | 0 |
| 1936/37 | 41 | 0 | 4 | 0 | 0 | 0 | 45 | 0 |
| 1937/38 | 35 | 0 | 2 | 0 | 3 | 0 | 40 | 0 |
| 1938/39 | 40 | 5 | 5 | 1 | 1 | 0 | 46 | 6 |
| | 225 | 5 | 24 | 1 | 5 | 0 | 254 | 6 |

**Honours at Everton**
Division 1 winner: 1938/39
FA Cup winner: 1933
Caps for Northern Ireland: 12
War-time appearances for the Football League: 1

# WARNEY CRESSWELL

*Warneford Cresswell was an elegant footballer,
heralded as the 'Prince of Full-backs'.*

Cresswell had moved from South Shields to Sunderland for £5,500 in 1922 and five years later joined Everton for about £7,000. He was recruited primarily to aid the fight against relegation and repaid the massive fee by helping the Toffees finish in twentieth position. During the following season, Everton underwent an amazing metamorphosis to win the Division 1 crown.

Cresswell was pivotal in the evolution of full-back play. His approach was considered somewhat unorthodox in the 1920's because he preferred to jockey opponents and usher them into impossible positions rather than rely on dour defence and resolute tackling. Cresswell's reputation for calm assurance and precise passing has been undimmed by the passage of time. The forerunner of the modern defender could play on either flank and provided the club with yeoman service for over a decade. His Goodison career was punctuated with numerous triumphs as well as several set-backs. Having forfeited their Division 1 status in 1929/30, Cresswell and his team-mates rode a wave of euphoria associated with winning the 1930/31 Division 2 title, 1931/32 Division 1 crown and 1933 FA Cup. He moved to Port Vale in 1936 and later managed Northampton Town.

Cresswell experienced his share of international action. He served in the armed forces during both World Wars and was detained as a Prisoner of War during the earlier conflict. On the footballing front, the England full-back gained nine international caps but only one of them was awarded during his time at Everton.

Born: South Shields, 1897
Height: 1.75 m (5 ft 9 in) Weight: 70.9 kg (11 st 2 lb)

|  | League | | FA Cup | | Other | | Total | |
|---|---|---|---|---|---|---|---|---|
|  | apps | goals | apps | goals | apps | goals | apps | goals |
| 1926/27 | 15 | 0 | 0 | 0 | 0 | 0 | 15 | 0 |
| 1927/28 | 36 | 0 | 2 | 0 | 0 | 0 | 38 | 0 |
| 1928/29 | 32 | 1 | 1 | 0 | 1 | 0 | 34 | 1 |
| 1929/30 | 30 | 0 | 0 | 0 | 0 | 0 | 30 | 0 |
| 1930/31 | 42 | 0 | 5 | 0 | 0 | 0 | 47 | 0 |
| 1931/32 | 40 | 0 | 0 | 0 | 0 | 0 | 40 | 0 |
| 1932/33 | 41 | 0 | 6 | 0 | 1 | 0 | 48 | 0 |
| 1933/34 | 25 | 0 | 1 | 0 | 0 | 0 | 26 | 0 |
| 1934/35 | 25 | 0 | 1 | 0 | 0 | 0 | 26 | 0 |
| 1935/36 | 4 | 0 | 0 | 0 | 0 | 0 | 4 | 0 |
|  | 290 | 1 | 16 | 0 | 2 | 0 | 308 | 1 |

**Honours at Everton**
Division 1 winner: 1927/28, 1931/32
Division 2 winner: 1930/31
FA Cup winner: 1933
Caps for England: 1
Appearances for the Football League: 2

# MR WILL CUFF

*Will Cuff was the guiding light at Everton
for over half a century.*

Cuff's association with the club stretched back to the pioneering days at Stanley Park, where he was an enthusiastic young supporter. The trustee and former choir-master of St Domingo chapel was appointed an Everton director in 1895 and helped steer the club through the minefields of early professionalism. Six years later he inherited the administrative duties from Richard Molyneux, who left for Brentford. In his role as Everton secretary between 1901-1919, Cuff was regarded as a skilled administrator and something of a footballing visionary by organising exhibition matches in South America.

Closer to home, he was instrumental in signing Bobby Parker and several other exponents of cultured football who helped carry off the Division 1 crown at the end of the 1914/15 season. Subsequently, Cuff served as club chairman between 1921-1938 and, along with Tom McIntosh and Ernest Green, completed the signing of another prolific goal-scorer - Dixie Dean from Tranmere Rovers. Their initiative was well-rewarded with two Division 1 titles and the FA Cup. Towards the end of Cuff's tenure as club chairman, Everton fielded another quality team spearheaded by Tommy Lawton. As a result, the Toffees bagged the 1938/39 championship and were poised to dominate English football before the outbreak of World War II hostilities.

Cuff was one of the most influential men in football administration and was elected to the Football League Management Committee in 1924. He became president of the Football League in 1939. Cuff held the post for 10 years and was the last to rule with an iron fist. However, his relationship with his Everton directors deteriorated after the war. His problems started when he opposed a constitutional change to allow one vote for each share owned, which he felt gave too much power to wealthy individuals. The ill-feeling peaked in 1946 when he was accused of wrongful use of proxies. He resigned two years later.

Few doubted that Everton had prospered during his tenures as an innovative chairman and an enthusiastic administrator. A lasting symbol of his unflagging dedication to the royal blue faith was the development of the first stadium with double-decker stands on all four sides. In parallel with his Goodison responsibilities, Cuff was a senior partner in a leading Merseyside law firm located in Castle Street. When he died in 1949, his funeral procession was reputed to have been the equivalent of two kilometres long.

Born: Liverpool, 1868
**Everton secretary/director/chairman:** 52 years

**Everton record during term**
League: 710 wins, 368 draws, 584 defeats

**Everton honours during term**
Division 1 champions: 1914/15, 1927/28, 1931/32
Division 1 runners-up: 1901/02, 1904/05, 1908/09, 1911/12
Division 2 champions: 1930/31
FA Cup winners: 1906, 1933
FA Cup runners-up: 1897, 1907

# DIXIE DEAN

*William Ralph Dean was the greatest marksman that football has ever known.*

Dean - who despised the nickname 'Dixie' - struck terror in the hearts of defenders and his prolific goal-scoring exploits carved out a special niche in sporting folklore. Signed from Tranmere Rovers for £3,000, Dean's performances were breath-taking, spine-tingling, and much more. He intimidated defences with his skills, courage and commitment and developed into the greatest centre-forward that football has ever known. Dean amassed 383 goals with the Toffees, including 37 hat-tricks, and averaged 0.885 goals per game.

His career peaked in 1928 when he set a record of 60 goals in 39 League games during the club's gallop to the Division 1 title - including 5 goals in one game against Manchester United. His tally for that championship season included another 40 goals in representative, charity and tour outings. The royal blue legend was idolised by football fans of all persuasions and universally revered for his sportsmanship. After an unparalleled career at Everton, Dean severed his ties with the club in 1938 and moved to Notts County for £3,000. He scored 3 goals in 11 games for the Meadow Lane-club before joining Sligo Rovers, where he bagged 11 goals in as many games. But his unbreakable spirit remained at his beloved Goodison Park and fittingly he died there in 1980.

Born: Birkenhead, 1907
Height: 1.78 m (5 ft 10 in)  Weight: 82.2 kg (12 st 13 lb)

|  | League | | FA Cup | | Others | | Total | |
|---|---|---|---|---|---|---|---|---|
|  | apps | goals | apps | goals | apps | goals | apps | goals |
| 1924/25 | 7 | 2 | 0 | 0 | 0 | 0 | 7 | 2 |
| 1925/26 | 38 | 32 | 2 | 1 | 0 | 0 | 40 | 33 |
| 1926/27 | 27 | 21 | 4 | 3 | 0 | 0 | 31 | 24 |
| 1927/28 | 39 | 60 | 2 | 3 | 0 | 0 | 41 | 63 |
| 1928/29 | 29 | 26 | 1 | 0 | 1 | 2 | 31 | 28 |
| 1929/30 | 25 | 23 | 2 | 2 | 0 | 0 | 27 | 25 |
| 1930/31 | 37 | 39 | 5 | 9 | 0 | 0 | 42 | 48 |
| 1931/32 | 38 | 45 | 1 | 1 | 0 | 0 | 39 | 46 |
| 1932/33 | 39 | 24 | 6 | 5 | 1 | 4 | 46 | 33 |
| 1933/34 | 12 | 9 | 0 | 0 | 0 | 0 | 12 | 9 |
| 1934/35 | 38 | 26 | 5 | 1 | 0 | 0 | 43 | 27 |
| 1935/36 | 29 | 17 | 0 | 0 | 0 | 0 | 29 | 17 |
| 1936/37 | 36 | 24 | 4 | 3 | 0 | 0 | 40 | 27 |
| 1937/38 | 5 | 1 | 0 | 0 | 0 | 0 | 5 | 1 |
|  | 399 | 349 | 32 | 28 | 2 | 6 | 433 | 383 |

### Honours at Everton
Division 1 winner:  1927/28, 1931/32
Division 2 winner:  1930/31
FA Cup winner:  1933
Caps for England:  16
Appearances for the Football League:  6

# JIMMY DUNN

*'Ginger' Dunn was a mercurial forward,
hailed as one of the 'Wembley Wizards'.*

Dunn was a product of the St Anthony's nursery in Govan, Glasgow. He was acquired by Everton from Hibernian for £5,000 in 1928, shortly after his success as a member of the famous Scotland team that demolished England by 5-1. Dunn tipped the scales at 66.7 kg and his diminutive firing-line colleagues, celebrated north of the border as the 'Wembley Wizards', included Alex James of Preston North End and Hughie Gallacher of Newcastle United.

Dunn thrilled the Goodison faithful with his array of footballing talents and was capable of turning any match with an inspired piece of skill. He tortured defenders with displays of speed and invention and proved to be the perfect foil for centre-forward Dixie Dean for over six seasons. As a result, Dunn bagged 49 goals for the Toffees but none was as important as the third goal in the eightieth minute of the 1933 FA Cup final against Manchester City. The little inside-right did not remember much about the highlight of his Everton career because he was knocked unconscious during the act of heading home Albert Geldard's looping corner.

In addition to his FA Cup final success, Dunn helped Everton win the Division 2 title in 1930/31 and the Division 1 championship in 1931/32. He also gained one Scotland cap during his Everton career, against Wales in 1928. After losing his first-team place to Nat Cunliffe, Dunn was transferred to Exeter City in 1935 and later turned out for Runcorn in the Cheshire County League.

Born: Glasgow, 1900
Height: 1.68 m (5 ft 6 in)  Weight: 66.7 kg (10 st 7 lb)

| | League apps | League goals | FA Cup apps | FA Cup goals | Others apps | Others goals | Total apps | Total goals |
|---|---|---|---|---|---|---|---|---|
| 1928/29 | 24 | 4 | 1 | 0 | 0 | 0 | 25 | 4 |
| 1929/30 | 12 | 0 | 1 | 0 | 0 | 0 | 13 | 0 |
| 1930/31 | 28 | 14 | 5 | 3 | 0 | 0 | 33 | 17 |
| 1931/32 | 22 | 10 | 0 | 0 | 0 | 0 | 22 | 10 |
| 1932/33 | 25 | 10 | 6 | 4 | 0 | 0 | 31 | 14 |
| 1933/34 | 23 | 4 | 1 | 0 | 1 | 0 | 25 | 4 |
| 1934/35 | 6 | 0 | 0 | 0 | 0 | 0 | 6 | 0 |
| | 140 | 42 | 14 | 7 | 1 | 0 | 155 | 49 |

**Honours at Everton**
Division 1 winner: 1931/32
Division 2 winner: 1930/31
FA Cup winner: 1933
Caps for Scotland: 1

# TOMMY EGLINGTON

*Tommy Eglington's unshakeable determination*
*returned Everton to the top flight.*

Eglington was recruited along with Peter Farrell from Shamrock Rovers in 1946. As a result of the £10,000 transaction, Everton gained the services of two dedicated club-men who missed very few games during their decade at Goodison Park. The Dublin-born outside-left was best known for tormenting more physically imposing defenders with his delicacy of touch and exhilarating change of pace. He also possessed stunning fire-power, highlighted by his five goals in a 7-1 thrashing of Doncaster Rovers.

Although Eglington was a potent match-winner, he struggled to keep Everton in Division 1 and after several close-shaves the club was relegated at the end of the 1949/50 campaign. But three seasons later, he scored several vital goals and did as much as any Everton player in returning them to the top flight. Ironically, he holds the somewhat dubious distinction of having played in more Division 2 games than any other Everton player.

A model professional for both club and countries, Eglington collected no major trophies during his Everton career but was honoured by both Eire and Northern Ireland. In fact, Eglington along with team-mate Farrell featured in the historic international game at Goodison Park in 1949 when Eire became the first foreign side to win on English soil. After more than a decade of stalwart service with the Toffees, he moved to Tranmere Rovers of Division 3 (North) in 1957. When his playing days were over, Eglington returned to Dublin to become the most famous butcher in the Emerald Isle.

Born: Dublin, 1923
Height: 1.70 m (5 ft 7 in) Weight: 65.4 kg (10 st 4 lb)

| | League apps | League goals | FA Cup apps | FA Cup goals | Total apps | Total goals |
|---|---|---|---|---|---|---|
| 1946/47 | 34 | 5 | 2 | 0 | 36 | 5 |
| 1947/48 | 29 | 3 | 5 | 1 | 34 | 4 |
| 1948/49 | 34 | 7 | 2 | 0 | 36 | 7 |
| 1949/50 | 34 | 1 | 5 | 0 | 39 | 1 |
| 1950/51 | 39 | 8 | 1 | 0 | 40 | 8 |
| 1951/52 | 38 | 8 | 2 | 0 | 40 | 8 |
| 1952/53 | 39 | 14 | 5 | 2 | 44 | 16 |
| 1953/54 | 41 | 11 | 3 | 1 | 44 | 12 |
| 1954/55 | 41 | 9 | 2 | 0 | 43 | 9 |
| 1955/56 | 38 | 8 | 4 | 2 | 42 | 10 |
| 1956/57 | 27 | 2 | 3 | 0 | 30 | 2 |
| | 394 | 76 | 34 | 6 | 428 | 82 |

**Honours at Everton**
Division 2 runner-up: 1953/54
Caps for Eire: 22
Caps for Northern Ireland: 6

# PETER FARRELL

*Peter Farrell made over 450 appearances
and was the most popular Evertonian of his era.*

Previously with Cabinteely United, Farrell arrived at Goodison via Shamrock Rovers along with left-winger Tommy Eglington. The sturdy wing-half was signed to fill the boots of Joe Mercer and embraced the unenviable assignment with his characteristic enthusiasm. He graced Goodison Park for more than a decade and, given that both Farrell and Eglington made over 400 first-team appearances, the club received tremendous value from their investment.

Farrell was a tough but honest competitor who tackled with conviction and wore his royal blue colours with immense pride. But despite his unwavering commitment, Everton struggled through the post-war football boom and were relegated at the conclusion of the 1949/50 season. After three seasons in the wilderness of Division 2 football, Farrell captained the club back to the top flight.

The Irish star was popular on and off the field, mixing freely with supporters in his friendly, down-to-earth manner. He played seven times for Northern Ireland as well as 26 times for Eire, and helped to make history when he scored for the Eire team that defeated England in 1949. Fittingly the venue for the Irish triumph was Goodison Park and, as a result, he entered the record books as the only internationalist ever to score an away goal at his home ground. Farrell teamed up again with his long-time friend Eglington in 1957 when he moved to the other side of the river to join Tranmere Rovers as player-manager for a fee of £2,500. He later had spells with Holyhead Town and Sligo Rovers.

Born: Dalkey, Dublin, 1922
Height: 1.73 m (5 ft 8 in)  Weight: 80.8 kg (12 st 10 lb)

|  | League apps | goals | FA Cup apps | goals | Total apps | goals |
|---|---|---|---|---|---|---|
| 1946/47 | 27 | 0 | 2 | 0 | 29 | 0 |
| 1947/48 | 38 | 2 | 3 | 1 | 41 | 3 |
| 1948/49 | 38 | 0 | 2 | 0 | 40 | 0 |
| 1949/50 | 41 | 2 | 5 | 0 | 46 | 2 |
| 1950/51 | 42 | 3 | 1 | 0 | 43 | 3 |
| 1951/52 | 40 | 0 | 2 | 0 | 42 | 0 |
| 1952/53 | 38 | 1 | 5 | 1 | 43 | 2 |
| 1953/54 | 39 | 1 | 3 | 0 | 42 | 1 |
| 1954/55 | 41 | 0 | 2 | 0 | 43 | 0 |
| 1955/56 | 42 | 1 | 4 | 1 | 46 | 2 |
| 1956/57 | 36 | 3 | 2 | 1 | 38 | 4 |
|  | 422 | 13 | 31 | 4 | 453 | 17 |

**Honours at Everton**
Division 2 runner-up: 1953/54
Caps for Eire: 26
Caps for Northern Ireland: 7

# WALLY FIELDING

*'Nobby' Fielding was the first Londoner
to be embraced by the Goodison faithful.*

Edmonton-born Fielding had broken into football as an amateur with Walthamstow Avenue and Charlton Athletic before the outbreak of hostilities. His big break came when he was spotted playing in Bari, Italy by club director Jack Sharp, who was serving as a major in the Royal Ordinance Corps. Fielding signed for the Toffees immediately after World War II. As a consequence, his arrival at Goodison Park was not without incident and his preference to sign professional forms with Everton resulted in furious exchanges with Charlton Athletic which lasted for months.

Although only slightly built, the master tactician ran the Everton engine-room with cool authority for over 13 seasons. Fielding was an intelligent footballer equipped with an aesthetic brand of perfectly-weighted passes. His other coruscating talents included mesmerising footwork and body-swerves which enabled him to waltz through massed ranks of defenders. Despite Fielding's immense skills and bubbling enthusiasm, the Toffees earned no meaningful honours during his tenure at Goodison. In fact, they were demoted to Division 2 in 1950 after surviving several narrow escapes.

The inside-right was selected to represent England against Scotland in the Bolton Disaster Fund match in 1946, but further international recognition eluded him. Fielding joined Southport as player-manager in 1959. He later returned south as trainer-coach at Luton and then youth coach at Watford.

Born: Edmonton, London, 1919
Height: 1.70 m (5 ft 7 in)  Weight: 68.1 kg (10 st 10 lb)

|  | League | | FA Cup | | Total | |
|---|---|---|---|---|---|---|
|  | apps | goals | apps | goals | apps | goals |
| 1945/46 | 0 | 0 | 2 | 0 | 2 | 0 |
| 1946/47 | 31 | 4 | 2 | 1 | 33 | 5 |
| 1947/48 | 33 | 8 | 5 | 2 | 38 | 10 |
| 1948/49 | 36 | 1 | 2 | 0 | 38 | 1 |
| 1949/50 | 14 | 0 | 3 | 0 | 17 | 0 |
| 1950/51 | 34 | 3 | 1 | 0 | 35 | 3 |
| 1951/52 | 37 | 4 | 2 | 0 | 39 | 4 |
| 1952/53 | 26 | 5 | 1 | 1 | 27 | 6 |
| 1953/54 | 39 | 5 | 3 | 0 | 42 | 5 |
| 1954/55 | 33 | 4 | 2 | 1 | 35 | 5 |
| 1955/56 | 29 | 3 | 4 | 0 | 33 | 3 |
| 1956/57 | 34 | 6 | 3 | 0 | 37 | 6 |
| 1957/58 | 24 | 4 | 0 | 0 | 24 | 4 |
| 1958/59 | 10 | 2 | 0 | 0 | 10 | 2 |
|  | 380 | 49 | 30 | 5 | 410 | 54 |

**Honours at Everton**
Division 2 runner-up: 1953/54

# TOM FLEETWOOD

*Tom Fleetwood's promising career*
*was savaged by the Great War.*

Originally a forward with non-League Rochdale, the Toxteth Park youngster cost £425 and provided gallant service as a half-back with Everton. Fleetwood developed into a mainstay in the Goodison set-up and was instrumental in the Toffees winning the Division 1 title in 1914/15. Although his career spanned over 12 seasons, his progress was interrupted by the outbreak of World War I. In total, he played 285 first-team games for Everton and also featured in 121 war-time fixtures in Lancashire Section tournaments. Indeed, he was reported to have played the best football of his career in the regional competitions organised during the hostilities.

Forceful on the ground and no slouch in the air, Fleetwood was a resourceful footballer. He occupied the right-half position throughout the 1914/15 championship campaign, but was often required to turn out for Everton at centre-half, full-back, inside-forward and centre-forward. As an emergency leader of the Goodison attack, Fleetwood displayed tremendous determination and vigour, and his tally of four goals in 15 outings was fewer than his efforts merited.

Fleetwood was selected to represent England in two Victory internationals in 1919. Both outings were against Scotland. Four years later he moved to Oldham Athletic and, upon his retirement, joined the Everton coaching and scouting staff.

Born: Liverpool, 1888
Height: 1.73 m (5 ft 8 in)  Weight: 75.4 kg (11 st 12 lb)

|  | League apps | League goals | FA Cup apps | FA Cup goals | Total apps | Total goals |
|---|---|---|---|---|---|---|
| 1910/11 | 8 | 1 | 0 | 0 | 8 | 1 |
| 1911/12 | 34 | 1 | 5 | 0 | 39 | 1 |
| 1912/13 | 28 | 1 | 2 | 1 | 30 | 2 |
| 1913/14 | 27 | 1 | 1 | 0 | 28 | 1 |
| 1914/15 | 35 | 2 | 5 | 0 | 40 | 2 |
| 1919/20 | 37 | 1 | 1 | 0 | 38 | 1 |
| 1920/21 | 39 | 1 | 4 | 0 | 43 | 1 |
| 1921/22 | 33 | 1 | 1 | 0 | 34 | 1 |
| 1922/23 | 23 | 0 | 2 | 0 | 25 | 0 |
|  | 264 | 9 | 21 | 1 | 285 | 10 |

**Honours at Everton**
Division 1 winner: 1914/15
Victory internationals: 2
Appearances for the Football League: 3
War-time appearances for the Football League: 2

# BERTIE FREEMAN

*Bertie Freeman smashed goal-scoring records wherever he played.*

Freeman had sojourns with Aston Manor, Aston Villa and Woolwich Arsenal before joining the Toffees for a fee of £350 in 1908. At Everton, he was employed as an out-and-out striker dependent on service from Goodison luminaries such as Jack Sharp and Sandy Young. Not surprisingly, he frequently found the target.

The tenacious centre-forward was full of hard running in the search of goals. He possessed a dangerous shot in both feet and was equally as lethal in the air. But more than anything, Freeman was blessed with a keen eye for an opening and a sixth sense of being in the right place at the right time. His uncanny instinct for tucking away half-chances resulted in 67 goals in a little over two full seasons with the club.

The pinnacle of his accomplishments was reached in the 1908/09 season when he established a Division 1 record by finding the net on 38 occasions in 37 League games. Despite his lethal finishing, Everton failed to clinch the Division 1 title and finished runners-up to Newcastle United. Freeman's achievement was equalled by Joe Smith of Bolton Wanderers in 1920/21 and was comprehensibly beaten by Dixie Dean in 1927/28. During his brief stay at Goodison, Freeman was awarded two caps by England. He also played for the Football League in 1909, netting four times against the Irish League.

The England centre-forward was sold to Burnley for £800 in 1911 and was replaced by Tom Browell. Freeman continued to score goals and was the League's leading marksman again in both 1911/12 and 1912/13. He also demonstrated a rare sense of occasion when he saddened part of Merseyside by grabbing the only goal in the 1914 English Cup final against Liverpool. Towards the end of his long and distinguished career, Freeman played non-League football with Wigan Borough and Kettering Town before retiring in 1924.

Born: Handsworth, Birmingham, 1885
Height: 1.73 m (5 ft 8 in)  Weight: 72.6 kg (11 st 6 lb)

|  | League apps | goals | FA Cup apps | goals | Total apps | goals |
|---|---|---|---|---|---|---|
| 1907/08 | 4 | 1 | 0 | 0 | 4 | 1 |
| 1908/09 | 37 | 38 | 1 | 0 | 38 | 38 |
| 1909/10 | 34 | 22 | 7 | 4 | 41 | 26 |
| 1910/11 | 11 | 2 | 0 | 0 | 11 | 2 |
|  | 86 | 63 | 8 | 4 | 94 | 67 |

**Honours at Everton**
Division 1 runner-up: 1908/09
Caps for England: 2
Appearances for the Football League: 1

# JIMMY GABRIEL

*Jimmy Gabriel was a versatile player
respected for his combative performances.*

The 19-year old golden boy of Scottish football was purchased by manager Johnny Carey from Dundee for £30,000 in 1960. Gabriel quickly made his mark at Everton with his resolute tackling and abrasive ball-winning skills. The right-half thrived on hard work and strained every sinew for the royal blue cause. He evolved into a versatile linchpin capable of turning defence into attack with his penetrating forays from mid-field.

Gabriel played an important part in Everton's success in capturing the Division 1 crown in 1962/63 and the FA Cup in 1966. He also contributed several exhilarating performances as an emergency centre-forward and bravely led the attack in Everton's first sortie into the European Cup against Internazionale in 1963. Surprisingly Gabriel was awarded only two Scotland international caps, shortly after his arrival at Goodison.

With the addition of young Howard Kendall from Preston North End in 1967, Gabriel moved on to Southampton and also enjoyed spells with Bournemouth and Brentford. He subsequently spent 10 years as a player-coach with Seattle Sounders (USA) before returning to the United Kingdom to work with Bournemouth as assistant-manager. Gabriel joined the Everton coaching staff in 1987 and served as caretaker-manager after the departures of Colin Harvey in 1990 and Howard Kendall in 1993. He emigrated to the United States in 1997.

Born: Dundee, 1940
Height: 1.78 m (5 ft 10 in)  Weight: 76.2 kg (12 st 0 lb)

| | League apps | League goals | FA Cup apps | FA Cup goals | Other apps | Other goals | Europe apps | Europe goals | Total apps | Total goals |
|---|---|---|---|---|---|---|---|---|---|---|
| 1959/60 | 8 | 0 | 0 | 0 | 0 | 0 | 0 | 0 | 8 | 0 |
| 1960/61 | 40 | 1 | 1 | 0 | 5 | 0 | 0 | 0 | 46 | 1 |
| 1961/62 | 42 | 6 | 3 | 0 | 0 | 0 | 0 | 0 | 45 | 6 |
| 1962/63 | 40 | 5 | 3 | 1 | 0 | 0 | 2 | 0 | 45 | 6 |
| 1963/64 | 33 | 5 | 5 | 1 | 1 | 1 | 1 | 0 | 40 | 7 |
| 1964/65 | 37 | 4 | 4 | 0 | 0 | 0 | 5 | 0 | 46 | 4 |
| 1965/66 | 24 | 6 | 6 | 0 | 0 | 0 | 3 | 1 | 33 | 7 |
| 1966/67 | 31/1 | 6 | 3 | 0 | 1 | 0 | 4 | 0 | 39/1 | 6 |
| | 255/1 | 33 | 25 | 2 | 7 | 1 | 15 | 1 | 302/1 | 37 |

**Honours at Everton**
Division 1 winner: 1962/63
FA Cup winner: 1966
Caps for Scotland: 2
Appearances for Scotland Under-23: 5

**Caretaker management record at Everton 1990/91 and 1993/94**
League: 1 win, 1 draw, 6 defeats

# FRED GEARY

*'Goal-a-game' Geary was the most talked-about marksman of his generation.*

Geary had turned out for Notts County, Notts Rangers and Grimsby Town before arriving at Anfield Road in 1889. With his knack for hitting the target, the 21-year old quickly established himself as one of the most prolific goal-poachers of the nineteenth century. The Everton spearhead was not built for the robust nature of the Victorian game and compensated for his physical limitations with electrifying bursts of speed and sharpness in and around the penalty area. Indeed, Geary was a phenomenal sprinter and went to extra ordinary lengths to improve his pace. He insisted on wearing football boots with the thinnest possible soles.

Ably supported up-front by the Chadwick-Milward partnership, Geary scored 86 goals in 98 games for the Toffees. With the centre-forward firing on all cylinders, Everton enjoyed a spell of impressive performances in which they won the Football League championship for the first time and also finished runners-up on two other occasions. Geary was an ever-present member of the 1890/91 championship team but was missing from the line-up for the 1893 English Cup final which Everton lost by 0-1 to Wolverhampton Wanderers.

The England star collected two international caps, grabbing a hat-trick in his debut against Ireland in 1890. However the arrival of free-scoring Jack Southworth from Blackburn Rovers undermined Geary's first-team place at Everton and he moved back to Anfield in 1895, joining Liverpool for a fee of £60. He subsequently chalked up 14 goals in 45 games for the Reds. Despite his sudden defection, Geary had already made his mark as the first Everton player to score at Goodison Park. He had found the target in the friendly against Bolton Wanderers in September 1892.

Born: Hyson Green, Nottingham, 1868
Height: 1.57 m (5 ft 2 in) Weight: 60.0 kg (9 st 6 lb)

|  | League apps | League goals | FA Cup apps | FA Cup goals | Total apps | Total goals |
|---|---|---|---|---|---|---|
| 1889/90 | 18 | 21 | 2 | 4 | 20 | 25 |
| 1890/91 | 22 | 20 | 1 | 0 | 23 | 20 |
| 1891/92 | 10 | 6 | 0 | 0 | 10 | 6 |
| 1892/93 | 24 | 19 | 3 | 4 | 27 | 23 |
| 1893/94 | 9 | 8 | 0 | 0 | 9 | 8 |
| 1894/95 | 8 | 4 | 1 | 0 | 9 | 4 |
|  | 91 | 78 | 7 | 8 | 98 | 86 |

**Honours at Everton**
League winner: 1890/91
League runner-up: 1889/90
Division 1 runner-up: 1894/95
FA Cup (English Cup) runner-up: 1893
Caps for England: 2
Appearances for the Football League: 2

# CHARLIE GEE

*Charlie Gee made a meteoric rise from junior football to international stardom.*

Gee launched his career with Reddish Green Wesleyans and moved to Stockport County in 1928. After only 25 League games with the Edgeley Park-club, he joined the recently relegated Toffees in Division 2 for £3,500. The young centre-half made his Goodison debut in January 1931 and his heroic efforts immediately bolstered the Everton defence. Gee blossomed under the benign eye of Warney Cresswell and made such an impact that Tommy Griffiths, the experienced Wales international pivot, was unable to retain his first-team place. Gee's progress was so dramatic that within 11 months he had represented England against Wales and Spain.

Gee was not reluctant to use his considerable strength to his advantage and matured into an uncomplicated and unforgiving defender at the core of the Goodison rearguard. His footballing abilities were underpinned by intelligent reading of the game as well as biting tackles. Gee's whole-hearted commitments towards the successful push for promotion in 1930/31 and the Division 1 championship in 1931/32 were well-appreciated by those of the royal blue persuasion. Unfortunately, he missed the 1933 FA Cup final as well as several international call-ups through knee injuries. In fact, he had to wait until 1936 to receive his third England cap.

Injuries continued to stymie his career and resulted in Gee conceding his place in the Everton first-team to TG Jones. After being side-lined for most of the 1938/39 championship campaign, he retired in 1940.

Born: Stockport, 1909
Height: 1.82 m (6 ft 0 in) Weight: 79.0 kg (12 st 6 lb)

|  | League apps | League goals | FA Cup apps | FA Cup goals | Other apps | Other goals | Total apps | Total goals |
|---|---|---|---|---|---|---|---|---|
| 1930/31 | 20 | 2 | 5 | 0 | 0 | 0 | 25 | 2 |
| 1931/32 | 38 | 0 | 1 | 0 | 0 | 0 | 39 | 0 |
| 1932/33 | 7 | 0 | 0 | 0 | 0 | 0 | 7 | 0 |
| 1933/34 | 29 | 0 | 0 | 0 | 1 | 0 | 30 | 0 |
| 1934/35 | 37 | 0 | 5 | 0 | 0 | 0 | 42 | 0 |
| 1935/36 | 9 | 0 | 0 | 0 | 0 | 0 | 9 | 0 |
| 1936/37 | 40 | 0 | 4 | 0 | 0 | 0 | 44 | 0 |
| 1937/38 | 14 | 0 | 0 | 0 | 0 | 0 | 14 | 0 |
| 1938/39 | 2 | 0 | 0 | 0 | 0 | 0 | 2 | 0 |
|  | 196 | 2 | 15 | 0 | 1 | 0 | 212 | 2 |

**Honours at Everton**
Division 1 winner: 1931/32
Division 2 winner: 1930/31
Caps for England: 3
Appearances for the Football League: 1

# ALBERT GELDARD

*Albert Geldard was endowed with fine technique*
*and devastating acceleration.*

Geldard was already something of a celebrity before he had even pulled on the famous royal blue of Everton. He had been a schoolboy prodigy - scoring 22 goals in one game for Whetley Lane School - and had turned out for Bradford Park Avenue Reserves as a 14-year old. The Bradford novice became the youngest player to appear in a peace-time League game when, at 15 years and 158 days, he debuted for the Yorkshire-club against Millwall in 1929.

Geldard continued to make swift progress in Division 2 and after 34 first-team outings was transferred to Everton for £4,000 in 1932. He was an exceptionally fast outside-right with magical footwork, who liked to wriggle his way through defences to provide the ammunition for Dixie Dean. Geldard played in the 1933 FA Cup final, replacing Ted Critchley who had scored the winner in the semi-final tie. He weathered the selection controversy and, along with Jimmy Stein on the other flank, provided the accurate crosses for Dean to successfully undermine the Manchester City defence.

The England international was awarded four caps, his first as a teenager against Italy in 1933, and was still in his prime when he joined Bolton Wanderers for a fee of around £7,000 in 1938. Geldard bowed out of the professional game shortly after World War II but came out of retirement for a brief spell with non-League Darwen. Renowned as an accomplished conjuror both on and off the pitch, he was a member of the Magic Circle.

Born: Bradford, 1914
Height: 1.70 m (5 ft 7 in)  Weight: 70.8 kg (11 st 2 lb)

|  | League | | FA Cup | | Other | | Total | |
|---|---|---|---|---|---|---|---|---|
|  | apps | goals | apps | goals | apps | goals | apps | goals |
| 1932/33 | 26 | 5 | 4 | 0 | 0 | 0 | 30 | 5 |
| 1933/34 | 24 | 5 | 0 | 0 | 1 | 0 | 25 | 5 |
| 1934/35 | 31 | 5 | 5 | 5 | 0 | 0 | 36 | 10 |
| 1935/36 | 39 | 7 | 1 | 1 | 0 | 0 | 40 | 8 |
| 1936/37 | 13 | 3 | 1 | 0 | 0 | 0 | 14 | 3 |
| 1937/38 | 34 | 6 | 1 | 0 | 1 | 0 | 36 | 6 |
|  | 167 | 31 | 12 | 6 | 2 | 0 | 181 | 37 |

**Honours at Everton**
FA Cup winner: 1933
Caps for England: 4
Appearances for the Football League: 1

# ANDY GRAY

*Andy Gray ignited team performances
with his courage and conviction.*

Gray breezed into Goodison in 1983 with an impressive pedigree tarnished by injuries and a spell of indifferent form. The Scotland international had enjoyed a sparkling early career and been voted PFA 'Player's Player' and PFA 'Young Player of the Year' in 1977. Previously with Dundee United and Aston Villa, the 27-year old super-star was lured away from ailing Wolverhampton Wanderers for the modest sum of £250,000. Four seasons earlier, he had commanded a British record fee of £1.469 million.

Gray turned out to be one of the club's most inspirational acquisitions. He notched 22 goals in 68 first-team outings, but statistics fail to reflect his true contributions. Along with team-mate Peter Reid, Gray transformed Everton in the mid-1980s. The Scotland star's passion and charisma lifted morale on the pitch, in the dressing room and among the Goodison congregation. Possibly the bravest striker of his era, Gray displayed his royal blue heart on his sleeve and won the majority of his physical battles against even the most formidable defenders. The fearless Glaswegian was an exhilarating sight when in full flight and scored vital goals in the 1984 FA Cup final victory over Watford and the 1985 European Cup-Winners' Cup triumph against Rapid Vienna.

His resurrection as an international striker was confirmed by his selection for Scotland against Iceland in 1985. However shortly afterwards, Gary Lineker was added to the Everton squad and the idol of the Goodison fans rejoined Aston Villa for £150,000. Subsequently, Gray played for Notts County, West Bromwich Albion, Glasgow Rangers and Cheltenham Town. After a brief stint as assistant-manager with Aston Villa, he became the leading television pundit on Sky Sports.

Born: Glasgow, 1955
Height: 1.83 m (6 ft 0 in) Weight: 74.0 kg (11 st 9 lb)

|  | League | | FA Cup | | Other | | Europe | | Total | |
|---|---|---|---|---|---|---|---|---|---|---|
|  | apps | goals | apps | goals | apps | goals | apps | goals | apps | goals |
| 1983/84 | 23 | 5 | 7/1 | 3 | 0 | 0 | 0 | 0 | 30/1 | 8 |
| 1984/85 | 21/5 | 9 | 7 | 0 | 0/1 | 0 | 3 | 5 | 31/6 | 14 |
|  | 44/5 | 14 | 14/1 | 3 | 0/1 | 1 | 3 | 5 | 61/7 | 22 |

**Honours at Everton**
European Cup-Winners' Cup winner: 1985
Division 1 winner: 1984/85
FA Cup winner: 1984
FA Cup runner-up: 1985
Caps for Scotland: 1

# HAROLD HARDMAN

*Harold Hardman was a gentleman footballer
and one of the leading amateurs of all time.*

Educated, athletic and a consummate gentleman, Hardman seemed too good to be true. The 21-year old amateur was signed by Everton from Blackpool in 1903 and made an immediate contribution towards enhancing the club's reputation for cultured and entertaining football. He replaced John Bell on the left-wing and blended perfectly with inside-forward Jimmy Settle.

Hardman was a pint-sized winger who made 156 appearances for the Toffees and participated in consecutive English Cup finals. Everton's victory over Newcastle United in the 1906 final meant that Hardman was only one of three amateurs to have won a cup winners' medal during the twentieth century. His fine turn of speed, precise passing and insatiable desire to be in the thick of the fray made him a great favourite at Goodison Park.

Hardman played for the sheer love of the game, usually with a smile on his face. Football was his hobby, possibly a refreshing change from practising law in Manchester, and he struggled to find time for serious training. Nevertheless, Hardman gave Everton faithful service and was rewarded with four full England caps to add to his 10 amateur international caps. He won a gold medal with the Great Britain soccer team at the 1908 Olympic Games and then departed to Manchester United. Later in his career, he turned out for Bradford City, Stoke and Northern Nomads. Hardman returned to Old Trafford and served as a club director for 36 years and as club chairman for another 14 years. He was also a member of the FA Council.

Born: Kirkmanshulme, Manchester, 1882
Height: 1.67 m (5 ft 6 in)  Weight: 60.5 kg (9 st 7 lb)

|  | League | | FA Cup | | Total | |
|---|---|---|---|---|---|---|
|  | apps | goals | apps | goals | apps | goals |
| **1903/04** | 26 | 5 | 0 | 0 | 26 | 5 |
| **1904/05** | 32 | 8 | 6 | 1 | 38 | 9 |
| **1905/06** | 31 | 6 | 6 | 2 | 37 | 8 |
| **1906/07** | 19 | 3 | 7 | 1 | 26 | 4 |
| **1907/08** | 22 | 3 | 7 | 0 | 29 | 3 |
|  | 130 | 25 | 26 | 4 | 156 | 29 |

**Honours at Everton**
Division 1 runner-up: 1904/05
FA Cup (English Cup) winner: 1906
FA Cup (English Cup) runner-up: 1907
Caps for England: 4
Amateur caps for England: 10
Appearances for the Football League: 1

# BRIAN HARRIS

*Brian Harris was a dedicated club-man*
*who filled nearly every position for Everton.*

Bebington-born Harris emerged from the relative obscurity of Port Sunlight in 1954. He made his Everton debut as an outside-right but was converted to a half-back by manager Johnny Carey. Harris contested the left-half position with Eire international Mick Meagan for five seasons before the introduction of Tony Kay from Sheffield Wednesday in 1962. However with the incarceration of Kay after the match-fixing trial, Harris recaptured his position in the Everton engine-room. His loyalty and resolute commitment to the royal blue cause won a special place in the hearts of even the more hard-to-please Goodison fans.

Harris was an all-round footballer of considerable athleticism and no little skill. He was respected as a crisp tackler and polished passer. In total, Harris clocked up over 350 games during his 12 seasons with the club and turned out for the first-team in seven different positions. Perhaps more than anything, he is remembered as an unselfish and consistent competitor who was influential in the early stages of the 1962/63 Division 1 championship drive and throughout the 1966 FA Cup run, which climaxed with a miraculous victory over Sheffield Wednesday at Wembley.

Harris was transferred to Cardiff City for £15,000 in 1966 and stayed in the principality to play for and manage Newport County. He later moved to Chepstow City and Cardiff City again. He wound down his career with a spell of scouting for Ipswich Town.

Born: Bebington, 1935
Height: 1.73 m (5 ft 8 in)  Weight: 73.6 kg (11 st 8 lb)

| | League apps | goals | FA Cup apps | goals | Other apps | goals | Europe apps | goals | Total apps | goals |
|---|---|---|---|---|---|---|---|---|---|---|
| 1955/56 | 20 | 2 | 4 | 1 | 0 | 0 | 0 | 0 | 24 | 3 |
| 1956/57 | 3 | 0 | 0 | 0 | 0 | 0 | 0 | 0 | 3 | 0 |
| 1957/58 | 30 | 6 | 3 | 0 | 0 | 0 | 0 | 0 | 33 | 6 |
| 1958/59 | 35 | 1 | 4 | 0 | 0 | 0 | 0 | 0 | 39 | 1 |
| 1959/60 | 32 | 1 | 1 | 0 | 0 | 0 | 0 | 0 | 33 | 1 |
| 1960/61 | 30 | 3 | 1 | 0 | 5 | 0 | 0 | 0 | 36 | 3 |
| 1961/62 | 33 | 1 | 3 | 0 | 0 | 0 | 0 | 0 | 36 | 1 |
| 1962/63 | 24 | 1 | 1 | 1 | 0 | 0 | 2 | 0 | 27 | 1 |
| 1963/64 | 28 | 3 | 5 | 2 | 0 | 0 | 2 | 0 | 35 | 5 |
| 1964/65 | 31 | 3 | 1 | 0 | 0 | 0 | 4 | 0 | 36 | 3 |
| 1965/66 | 40 | 2 | 8 | 0 | 0 | 0 | 4 | 2 | 52 | 4 |
| 1966/67 | 4 | 0 | 0 | 0 | 0 | 0 | 0 | 0 | 4 | 0 |
| | 310 | 23 | 31 | 4 | 5 | 0 | 12 | 2 | 358 | 29 |

**Honours at Everton**
Division 1 winner: 1962/63
FA Cup winner: 1966

# HUNTER HART

*Hunter Hart was rated as one of the best defenders of his generation.*

The left-half was recruited from Airdrieonians for £4,000 in 1922 to bolster Everton's defence. His diligent efforts inspired a narrow escape from relegation during his first season, with Everton finishing in twentieth position. Hardly a colossus at 1.75 m, Hart was a commanding defender with a never-say-die attitude. He tackled with grit and determination and distributed the ball with efficiency and precision.

Hart played over 300 games for Everton and experienced numerous highs and lows during his Goodison career. After another flirtation with relegation in 1925/26, he replaced Neil McBain at the heart of the Everton defence and was appointed club captain. The club's fortunes changed dramatically over the next 12 months as Dixie Dean spearheaded the club through the record-breaking 1927/28 League championship campaign. Unfortunately the success was fleeting and Everton tumbled to eighteenth position by the end of the following season.

In an attempt to strengthen the defence, Hart reverted to left-half to accommodate Tommy Griffiths at centre-half. Sadly, the change was unproductive. The Toffees were relegated to Division 2 in 1929/30 and Hart decided to hang up his boots. Although he had represented the Scottish League during his early days at Airdrieonians, his abilities were never fully appreciated by Scotland. He joined the Goodison office staff and was appointed assistant-secretary in 1936.

Born: Glasgow, 1897
Height: 1.75 m (5 ft 9 in) Weight: 73.1 kg (11 st 7 lb)

| | League | | FA Cup | | Others | | Total | |
|---|---|---|---|---|---|---|---|---|
| | apps | goals | apps | goals | apps | goals | apps | goals |
| 1921/22 | 17 | 0 | 0 | 0 | 0 | 0 | 17 | 0 |
| 1922/23 | 40 | 1 | 2 | 0 | 0 | 0 | 42 | 1 |
| 1923/24 | 42 | 2 | 1 | 0 | 0 | 0 | 43 | 2 |
| 1924/25 | 24 | 0 | 0 | 0 | 0 | 0 | 24 | 0 |
| 1925/26 | 26 | 0 | 0 | 0 | 0 | 0 | 26 | 0 |
| 1926/27 | 39 | 1 | 3 | 0 | 0 | 0 | 42 | 1 |
| 1927/28 | 41 | 1 | 2 | 0 | 0 | 0 | 43 | 1 |
| 1928/29 | 40 | 0 | 1 | 0 | 1 | 0 | 42 | 0 |
| 1929/30 | 20 | 0 | 2 | 0 | 0 | 0 | 22 | 0 |
| | 289 | 5 | 11 | 0 | 1 | 0 | 301 | 5 |

**Honours at Everton**
Division 1 winner: 1927/28

# COLIN HARVEY

*Colin Harvey was a mid-field maestro*
*with immaculate ball skills.*

Harvey graduated through the club's junior teams and was baptised by fire as an 18-year old in a 1964 European Cup tie at Milan. He was an elegant footballer and delighted the followers of the royal blue persuasion with his sublime ball control, imaginative passing, fearless tackling and prodigious workrate. Nicknamed 'The White Pele', the Everton play-maker featured in the most accomplished mid-field trio ever fielded by a British club. Kendall, Harvey & Ball were near-invincible and romped away with the 1969/70 title. Amazingly their reign was ephemeral, the decline being exacerbated by Harvey's eye complaints and hip injuries.

Harvey moved to Sheffield Wednesday in 1974 for £70,000 but, at the conclusion of his playing career, returned to his spiritual home as a coach. He made vast contributions towards the club's success in the mid-1980s and was elevated to Everton manager in 1987. Unfortunately, his term was an undistinguished one. Harvey continued his coaching career at Oldham Athletic and Burnley before returning to Everton as youth coach. His new charges carried off the FA Youth Cup in 1998.

Born: Liverpool, 1944
Height: 1.70 m (5 ft 7 in)  Weight: 70.0 kg (11 st 0 lb)

| | League apps | League goals | FA Cup apps | FA Cup goals | Other apps | Other goals | Europe apps | Europe goals | Total apps | Total goals |
|---|---|---|---|---|---|---|---|---|---|---|
| 1963/64 | 2 | 0 | 0 | 0 | 0 | 0 | 1 | 0 | 3 | 0 |
| 1964/65 | 32 | 2 | 4 | 1 | 0 | 0 | 4 | 2 | 40 | 5 |
| 1965/66 | 40 | 1 | 8 | 1 | 0 | 0 | 4 | 0 | 52 | 2 |
| 1966/67 | 42 | 1 | 6 | 0 | 1 | 0 | 4 | 0 | 53 | 1 |
| 1967/68 | 34 | 0 | 4 | 0 | 2 | 0 | 0 | 0 | 40 | 0 |
| 1968/69 | 36 | 4 | 4 | 0 | 4 | 0 | 0 | 0 | 44 | 4 |
| 1969/70 | 35 | 3 | 0 | 0 | 3 | 0 | 0 | 0 | 38 | 3 |
| 1970/71 | 36 | 2 | 5 | 1 | 1 | 0 | 6 | 0 | 48 | 3 |
| 1971/72 | 17 | 3 | 3 | 1 | 0 | 0 | 0 | 0 | 20 | 4 |
| 1972/73 | 24/2 | 0 | 0 | 0 | 1 | 0 | 0 | 0 | 25/2 | 0 |
| 1973/74 | 15/2 | 1 | 0 | 0 | 0/1 | 0 | 0 | 0 | 15/3 | 1 |
| 1974/75 | 4 | 1 | 0 | 0 | 0 | 0 | 0 | 0 | 4 | 1 |
| | 317/4 | 18 | 34 | 4 | 12/1 | 0 | 19 | 2 | 382/5 | 24 |

### Honours at Everton
Division 1 winner: 1969/70
FA Cup winner: 1966
FA Cup runner-up: 1968
Caps for England: 1
Caps for England Under-23: 5
Appearances for the Football League: 3

### Management record at Everton 1987/88-1990/91
League: 51 wins, 37 draws, 38 defeats
FA Cup runners-up: 1989
Simod Cup runners-up: 1987/88

# ADRIAN HEATH

*'Inchy' Heath made a giant-size contribution to Everton's success in the 1980s.*

Nurtured by Stoke City, the 20-year old was acquired for a club record fee of £700,000 in 1982. Heath boasted tremendous ball control, immense courage and a devastating turn of speed. His subtlety of mind and movement meant that he could be deployed as an out-and-out striker, hover behind the front-men or forage in mid-field. Although only 1.64 m tall, Heath was equal to the most daunting of physical challenges. Many royal blue fans anointed the pocket dynamo as Everton's post-war saviour after his opportunism in snatching a late equaliser in the fifth round of the Milk Cup at Oxford revived the flagging fortunes of the manager and the club. Consequently Everton grew in confidence and progressed to two Wembley finals in 1984, including the first all-Merseyside showdown.

During the following season his career was undermined by a serious knee injury as his colleagues strove toward the 1984/85 title and European success. Heath recovered to contribute vital goals alongside Gary Lineker and Graeme Sharp. Not long after the 1986/87 championship triumph, he was transferred to Espanol (Spain) for £650,000 and later played for Aston Villa, Manchester City and Stoke City. After a brief stint as player-coach at Sheffield United, Heath was appointed manager at Burnley. The careers of Heath and Kendall crossed on several occasions - at Stoke City, Manchester City and Sheffield United. In 1997, he was re-united with Howard Kendall at Everton for a short engagement as assistant-manager. Most recently he joined the coaching staff at Sunderland

Born: Stoke on Trent, 1961
Height: 1.64 m (5 ft 5 in)  Weight: 64.0 kg (10 st 1 lb)

| | League apps | goals | FA Cup apps | goals | Other apps | goals | Europe apps | goals | Total apps | goals |
|---|---|---|---|---|---|---|---|---|---|---|
| 1981/82 | 22 | 6 | 0 | 0 | 0 | 0 | 0 | 0 | 22 | 6 |
| 1982/83 | 37/1 | 10 | 5 | 1 | 4 | 0 | 0 | 0 | 46/1 | 11 |
| 1983/84 | 36 | 12 | 7 | 2 | 11 | 4 | 0 | 0 | 54 | 18 |
| 1984/85 | 17 | 11 | 0 | 0 | 5 | 1 | 4 | 1 | 26 | 13 |
| 1985/86 | 24/12 | 10 | 2/4 | 2 | 9/1 | 3 | 0 | 0 | 35/17 | 15 |
| 1986/87 | 41 | 11 | 3 | 0 | 8 | 6 | 0 | 0 | 52 | 17 |
| 1987/88 | 23/6 | 9 | 7/1 | 1 | 7/2 | 2 | 0 | 0 | 37/9 | 12 |
| 1988/89 | 6/1 | 2 | 0 | 0 | 2/1 | 0 | 0 | 0 | 8/2 | 2 |
| | 206/20 | 71 | 24/5 | 6 | 46/4 | 16 | 4 | 1 | 280/29 | 94 |

**Honours at Everton**
Division 1 winner: 1984/85, 1986/87
Division 1 runner-up: 1985/86
FA Cup winner: 1984
FA Cup runner-up: 1986
Milk Cup runner-up: 1983/84
Screen Sport Super Cup runner-up: 1985/86
Caps for England 'B': 1
Caps for England Under-21: 3

# DAVE HICKSON

*Dave Hickson was a no-nonsense forward with his own brand of dashing football.*

Shortly after his arrival at Goodison Park from Ellesmere Port Town, Hickson struck up a promising understanding with John Willie Parker. Both forwards were nurtured in the Central League team to hone their predatory skills. Hickson developed thunderous firepower in both feet and displayed excellent mobility, superior heading skills and immense courage. Their goal-scoring partnership went from strength-to-strength and their goals helped to propel Everton out of Division 2 in 1953/54.

Nicknamed the 'Cannonball Kid', Hickson was respected for his whole-hearted approach to the game. Quiet and unassuming off the field, he was transformed into an intimidating gladiator when attired in his beloved royal blue. In fact, the swashbuckling centre-forward shed blood, sweat and tears for Everton and gained cult status with the Goodison faithful.

On occasions his unrestrained enthusiasm and fiery temperament got him into disciplinary trouble and prompted numerous transfer transactions. Everton fans were shocked when Hickson was sold to Aston Villa for £17,500 in 1955 and shortly afterwards moved on to Huddersfield Town. But they rejoiced when he returned for a second spell at Goodison Park for a bargain fee of £7,500, only to be flabbergasted by his defection to Liverpool for £12,000 two years later. Subsequently, Hickson enjoyed engagements with non-League Cambridge United, Bury, Tranmere Rovers and Ballymena United.

Although he holds the distinction of being the only senior player to have turned out for Everton, Liverpool and Tranmere Rovers, Hickson remains one of the most proud Evertonians of all time.

Born: Salford, 1929
Height: 1.78 m (5 ft 10 in)  Weight: 80.8 kg (12 st 10 lb)

|  | League apps | League goals | FA Cup apps | FA Cup goals | Total apps | Total goals |
|---|---|---|---|---|---|---|
| 1951/52 | 31 | 14 | 2 | 0 | 33 | 14 |
| 1952/53 | 27 | 12 | 5 | 4 | 32 | 16 |
| 1953/54 | 40 | 25 | 3 | 3 | 43 | 28 |
| 1954/55 | 39 | 12 | 2 | 1 | 41 | 13 |
| 1955/56 | 2 | 0 | 0 | 0 | 2 | 0 |
| 1957/58 | 35 | 9 | 2 | 3 | 37 | 12 |
| 1958/59 | 39 | 17 | 4 | 5 | 43 | 22 |
| 1959/60 | 12 | 6 | 0 | 0 | 12 | 6 |
|  | 225 | 95 | 18 | 16 | 243 | 111 |

**Honours at Everton**
Division 2 runner-up: 1953/54

# JOHNNY HOLT

*Johnny Holt was an unyielding defender*
*and Everton's first internationalist.*

Although only 1.63 m and 61.3 kg, Holt was an authoritative figure and a mainstay in the Everton defence before the turn of the century. Labelled the 'Little Devil' by the fans who worshiped him, the uncompromising centre-half was surprisingly powerful in the air and capable of out-jumping much taller opponents. Holt was also renowned as a determined tackler, skilled at man-marking and shackling adversaries. He loved to entertain spectators and, as a consequence of his unorthodox trickery, possibly no defender in the history of the club has intentionally raised more laughs from the Everton crowd.

Previously with Church, a leading club in the Blackburn area, Holt joined Everton from their local rivals Bootle just in time for the start of the inaugural season of the Football League. Alongside Richard Boyle and Billy Stewart in the half-back line, he was influential in the early successes of the Anfield-based club. Holt was a member of Everton's first championship side in 1890/91 and also appeared in two English Cup finals in 1893 and 1897. But despite his heroic efforts, Everton finished runners-up on both occasions.

Holt was the club's first internationalist and went on to play for England on nine occasions. He was blooded against Wales at Wrexham on March 15, 1890. Fred Geary also represented England against Ireland in Belfast on the same day but at a later kick off time. Holt played for the Football League before moving to Reading of the Southern League in 1898.

Born: Blackburn, 1865
Height: 1.63 m (5 ft 4 in)  Weight: 61.3 kg (9 st 9 lb)

| | League apps | League goals | FA Cup apps | FA Cup goals | Total apps | Total goals |
|---|---|---|---|---|---|---|
| 1888/89 | 17 | 0 | 0 | 0 | 17 | 0 |
| 1889/90 | 21 | 1 | 2 | 0 | 23 | 1 |
| 1890/91 | 21 | 1 | 1 | 0 | 22 | 1 |
| 1891/92 | 21 | 0 | 1 | 0 | 22 | 0 |
| 1892/93 | 26 | 0 | 7 | 0 | 33 | 0 |
| 1893/94 | 26 | 0 | 1 | 0 | 27 | 0 |
| 1894/95 | 27 | 0 | 3 | 0 | 30 | 0 |
| 1895/96 | 14 | 0 | 2 | 0 | 16 | 0 |
| 1896/97 | 25 | 1 | 5 | 1 | 30 | 2 |
| 1897/98 | 27 | 0 | 5 | 0 | 32 | 0 |
| | 225 | 3 | 27 | 1 | 252 | 4 |

**Honours at Everton**
League winner: 1890/91
League runner-up: 1889/90
Division 1 runner-up: 1894/95
FA Cup (English Cup) runner-up: 1893, 1897
Caps for England: 9
Appearances for the Football League: 1

# JOHN HURST

*John Hurst was the most under-rated*
*defender of his generation.*

A product of Harry Catterick's youth development initiatives, the Blackpool-born inside-forward won an FA Youth Cup winners' medal in 1965. Shortly afterwards he was converted into a defender and won a regular place alongside England centre-half Brian Labone at the heart of the Everton rearguard. Hurst matured into a cultured defender in the glory years of the late 1960s.

Probably the most unassuming man in the Everton dressing-room, Hurst was an exemplary professional who shunned the limelight. Renowned as an intelligent reader of the game, he made good use of his tremendous ball skills. He was ice-cool under pressure and linked-up constructively with his star-studded mid-field to reinforce the reputation of the Goodison School of Science for entertaining play. Although he was awarded nine Under-23 caps by England, Hurst was unlucky not to gain full international honours.

Hurst holds the distinction of being Everton's first-ever substitute when he replaced Fred Pickering against Stoke City in 1965. The dedicated club-man and veteran of more than 400 outings with Everton moved to Oldham Athletic in 1976. He returned to Goodison for a brief spell as youth coach in the 1990s.

Born: Blackpool, 1947
Height: 1.78 m (5 ft 10 in)  Weight: 78.5 kg (12 st 4 lb)

| | League apps | League goals | FA Cup apps | FA Cup goals | Other apps | Other goals | Europe apps | Europe goals | Total apps | Total goals |
|---|---|---|---|---|---|---|---|---|---|---|
| 1965/66 | 19/4 | 2 | 0 | 0 | 0 | 0 | 0 | 0 | 19/4 | 2 |
| 1966/67 | 23/2 | 2 | 6 | 0 | 0 | 0 | 0 | 0 | 29/2 | 2 |
| 1967/68 | 40 | 5 | 5 | 0 | 2 | 1 | 0 | 0 | 47 | 6 |
| 1968/69 | 42 | 7 | 5 | 2 | 4 | 0 | 0 | 0 | 51 | 9 |
| 1969/70 | 42 | 5 | 1 | 0 | 3 | 0 | 0 | 0 | 46 | 5 |
| 1970/71 | 40 | 3 | 5 | 0 | 1 | 0 | 6 | 0 | 52 | 3 |
| 1971/72 | 28/1 | 0 | 1/2 | 1 | 1 | 0 | 0 | 0 | 30/3 | 1 |
| 1972/73 | 28/1 | 1 | 2 | 0 | 0 | 0 | 0 | 0 | 30/1 | 1 |
| 1973/74 | 39 | 3 | 3 | 1 | 4 | 0 | 0 | 0 | 46 | 4 |
| 1974/75 | 29/2 | 1 | 1 | 0 | 0 | 0 | 0 | 0 | 30/2 | 1 |
| 1975/76 | 6/3 | 0 | 1 | 0 | 1 | 0 | 0/1 | 0 | 8/4 | 0 |
| | 336/13 | 29 | 30/2 | 4 | 16 | 1 | 6/1 | 0 | 388/16 | 34 |

**Honours at Everton**
Division 1 winner: 1969/70
FA Cup runner-up: 1968
Caps for England Under-23: 9

# TOMMY JONES

*Thomas Edwin Jones was respected for his*
*fair-play and commitment to Everton.*

Jones made spectacular progress through the club's junior teams. After one game for the 'A' team and another for the reserves, he made his senior debut in 1950. Jones honed his skills at full-back but was converted to a central defender when Everton sought to replace TG Jones. Though a less sophisticated footballer than his illustrious namesake, TE Jones matured into a reliable defender and was appointed club captain in 1957. He exuded decency both on and off the pitch throughout his playing career and his impeccable sportsmanship was legendary.

Possessing formidable strength in the tackle and power in the air, he developed into Everton's first-choice centre-half for most of the 1950s. However, the commanding pivot lacked the streak of ruthlessness that runs through many top international defenders. Even though he failed to reach international stardom, Jones was rewarded with the captaincy of the FA side which toured Ghana and Nigeria in 1958.

He played most of his games at centre-half but reverted to left-back towards the end of his Goodison career to accommodate the advancement of young Brian Labone. A shattered kneecap forced him to retire in 1961 after making more than 400 first-team appearances for his only club.

Born: Liverpool, 1930
Height: 1.78 m (5 ft 10 in)  Weight: 80.0 kg (12 st 8 lb)

| | League apps | League goals | FA Cup apps | FA Cup goals | Other apps | Other goals | Total apps | Total goals |
|---|---|---|---|---|---|---|---|---|
| 1950/51 | 30 | 0 | 1 | 0 | 0 | 0 | 31 | 0 |
| 1951/52 | 37 | 0 | 0 | 0 | 0 | 0 | 37 | 0 |
| 1952/53 | 42 | 0 | 5 | 0 | 0 | 0 | 47 | 0 |
| 1953/54 | 37 | 1 | 3 | 0 | 0 | 0 | 40 | 1 |
| 1954/55 | 41 | 4 | 2 | 0 | 0 | 0 | 43 | 4 |
| 1955/56 | 39 | 2 | 4 | 0 | 0 | 0 | 43 | 2 |
| 1956/57 | 39 | 3 | 1 | 0 | 0 | 0 | 40 | 3 |
| 1957/58 | 31 | 0 | 3 | 0 | 0 | 0 | 34 | 0 |
| 1958/59 | 38 | 4 | 4 | 0 | 0 | 0 | 42 | 4 |
| 1959/60 | 35 | 0 | 1 | 0 | 0 | 0 | 36 | 0 |
| 1960/61 | 13 | 0 | 1 | 0 | 3 | 0 | 17 | 0 |
| 1961/62 | 1 | 0 | 0 | 0 | 0 | 0 | 1 | 0 |
| | 383 | 14 | 25 | 0 | 3 | 0 | 411 | 14 |

**Honours at Everton**
Division 2 runner-up: 1953/54

# TG JONES

*Thomas Gwynfor Jones was acclaimed as the most cultured British defender of all time.*

TG Jones broke into the Wrexham team as a 16-year old and after only half a dozen League games was signed by Everton for £3,000. His aristocratic style of play immediately gained the approval of the Goodison fans. Jones was strong in the air, crisp in the tackle and calm in a crisis, but his true quality was reflected by his delicate ball skills on the ground. He developed into a polished centre-half with the uncommon ability and confidence to stroke the ball around when under pressure.

Jones was also a determined competitor and, along with his young team-mates Tommy Lawton and Joe Mercer, made a significant contribution toward Everton's successful League championship campaign in 1938/39. Sadly, Jones managed to complete only two seasons in the top flight before his career was interrupted by World War II. After the cessation of hostilities, he played fewer than 100 post-war League games for Everton before retiring from first-class football in 1950.

The sophisticated defender made 17 appearances for Wales. But his reputation spread beyond the boundaries of the principality and Everton tentatively accepted a bid of £15,000 from AS Roma (Italy) for Jones in 1947. However, the transfer negotiations collapsed due to foreign exchange issues. He eventually left the club in 1950 and served Pwllheli as player-manager. He subsequently managed Bangor City and Rhyl in the Welsh League.

Born: Connah's Quay, 1917
Height: 1.86 m (6 ft 1 in)  Weight: 87.2 kg (13 st 10 lb)

| | League apps | League goals | FA Cup apps | FA Cup goals | Other apps | Other goals | Total apps | Total goals |
|---|---|---|---|---|---|---|---|---|
| 1936/37 | 1 | 0 | 0 | 0 | 0 | 0 | 1 | 0 |
| 1937/38 | 28 | 0 | 2 | 0 | 3 | 0 | 33 | 0 |
| 1938/39 | 39 | 0 | 5 | 0 | 1 | 0 | 45 | 0 |
| 1946/47 | 22 | 3 | 1 | 1 | 0 | 0 | 23 | 4 |
| 1947/48 | 24 | 1 | 0 | 0 | 0 | 0 | 24 | 1 |
| 1948/49 | 37 | 0 | 2 | 0 | 0 | 0 | 39 | 0 |
| 1949/50 | 14 | 0 | 0 | 0 | 0 | 0 | 14 | 0 |
| | 165 | 4 | 10 | 1 | 4 | 0 | 179 | 5 |

**Honours at Everton**
Division 1 winner: 1938/39
Caps for Wales: 17
War-time internationals: 11

# HOWARD KENDALL

*Howard Kendall was a stylish footballer
and the club's most successful manager.*

Kendall was the youngest player, at 17 years 345 days, to appear in an FA Cup final when he represented Preston North End in 1964. Two years later he moved to Everton for £80,000. Renowned for his perceptive passing and brisk tackling, Kendall was an integral part of the Everton mid-field trinity whose fluid football dominated the late-1960s. Although included in the 1972 England squad against Yugoslavia, he was never capped by his country. Kendall and full-back Archie Styles were traded to Birmingham City in 1974 in the deal which brought Bob Latchford to Goodison.

After gaining coaching experience at Stoke City and Blackburn Rovers, Kendall was charged with guiding Everton out of the shadows of their red neighbours. His teams captured two Division 1 titles and the club's first European trophy, and also appeared in five Wembley finals. He was voted Bell's Whisky 'Manager of the Year' on two occasions but resigned in 1987 to manage Athletic Bilbao (Spain). Kendall took over the Goodison reigns again in 1990 and 1997. His other travels have taken him to Xanthi (Greece), Manchester City, Notts County, Sheffield United and Ethanikos Piraeus (Greece).

Born: Ryton on Tyne, 1946
Height: 1.73 m (5 ft 8 in) Weight: 70.0 kg (11 st 0 lb)

| | League apps | League goals | FA Cup apps | FA Cup goals | Other apps | Other goals | Europe apps | Europe goals | Total apps | Total goals |
|---|---|---|---|---|---|---|---|---|---|---|
| 1966/67 | 4 | 0 | 0 | 0 | 0 | 0 | 0 | 0 | 4 | 0 |
| 1967/78 | 38 | 6 | 6 | 1 | 2 | 2 | 0 | 0 | 46 | 9 |
| 1968/69 | 28/1 | 1 | 3 | 0 | 4 | 0 | 0 | 0 | 35/1 | 1 |
| 1969/70 | 36 | 4 | 1 | 0 | 4 | 1 | 0 | 0 | 41 | 5 |
| 1970/71 | 40 | 2 | 5 | 2 | 1 | 1 | 6 | 2 | 52 | 7 |
| 1971/72 | 34/2 | 4 | 4 | 0 | 0 | 0 | 0 | 0 | 38/2 | 4 |
| 1972/73 | 40 | 4 | 2 | 0 | 1 | 0 | 0 | 0 | 43 | 4 |
| 1973/74 | 7 | 0 | 1 | 0 | 0 | 0 | 0 | 0 | 8 | 0 |
| 1981/82 | 4 | 0 | 1 | 0 | 1 | 0 | 0 | 0 | 6 | 0 |
| | 231/3 | 21 | 23 | 3 | 13 | 4 | 6 | 2 | 273/3 | 30 |

**Honours at Everton**
Division 1 winner: 1969/70
FA Cup runner-up: 1968
Caps for England Under-23: 6

**Management record at Everton 1981/82-1986/87, 1990/91-1993/94, 1997/98**
League: 207 wins, 123 draws, 147 defeats
European Cup-Winners' Cup winners: 1984/85
Division 1 champions: 1984/85, 1986/87
Division 1 runners-up: 1985/86
FA Cup winners: 1984
FA Cup runners-up: 1985, 1986
Milk Cup runners-up: 1983/84
Zenith Data Systems Cup runners-up: 1990/91
Screen Sport Super Cup runners-up: 1985/86

# ROGER KENYON

*Roger Kenyon stamped his authority*
*on every game in which he played.*

Kenyon launched his Goodison career in 1966 and within two years had matured into an important member of the first-team squad. The rugged defender embraced the unenviable challenge of replacing Brian Labone and developed into a staunch combatant at the centre of the Everton rearguard. Nicknamed the 'Assassin' by his team-mates, Kenyon was a top-class defender cast from a different mould than his predecessor and was respected for his scything tackles, sound distribution and impressive turn of speed. He was the model of consistency and was committed to the royal blue cause. Unfortunately, his career was undermined by injuries sustained in a car accident in 1974.

Kenyon collected no silverware with Everton. He came closest in 1977 when the Toffees lost to Aston Villa in the final minute of extra time of the second replay of the Football League Cup final. In the first replay at Hillsborough, he had the dubious distinction of putting through his own goal. Also Kenyon was arguably the unluckiest player not to have received international recognition. He was selected as substitute for England on several occasions but was confined to the bench and was never given the chance to stretch his legs on the big stage.

After battling through a dozen campaigns with the Toffees, the central defender moved to Vancouver Whitecaps (Canada) and won the NASL championship. Kenyon also played for Bristol City before retiring in 1980.

Born: Blackpool, 1949
Height: 1.83 m (6 ft 0 in)  Weight: 74.5 kg (11 st 10 lb)

| | League apps | goals | FA Cup apps | goals | Other apps | goals | Europe apps | goals | Total apps | goals |
|---|---|---|---|---|---|---|---|---|---|---|
| 1967/68 | 12/4 | 0 | 2 | 0 | 0 | 0 | 0 | 0 | 14/4 | 0 |
| 1968/69 | 4/3 | 0 | 0/1 | 0 | 0/2 | 0 | 0 | 0 | 4/6 | 0 |
| 1969/70 | 8/1 | 0 | 0 | 0 | 0/1 | 0 | 0 | 0 | 8/2 | 0 |
| 1970/71 | 28/2 | 0 | 2 | 0 | 0 | 0 | 4 | 0 | 34/2 | 0 |
| 1971/72 | 34/2 | 0 | 3 | 1 | 1 | 0 | 0 | 0 | 38/2 | 1 |
| 1972/73 | 40 | 2 | 2 | 0 | 1 | 0 | 0 | 0 | 43 | 2 |
| 1973/74 | 36 | 2 | 1 | 0 | 4 | 0 | 0 | 0 | 41 | 2 |
| 1974/75 | 40 | 0 | 2 | 1 | 2 | 0 | 0 | 0 | 44 | 1 |
| 1975/76 | 28/2 | 1 | 1 | 0 | 4 | 1 | 2 | 0 | 35/2 | 2 |
| 1976/77 | 14 | 1 | 1 | 0 | 3 | 0 | 0 | 0 | 18 | 1 |
| 1977/78 | 7 | 0 | 1 | 0 | 0 | 0 | 0 | 0 | 8 | 0 |
| 1978/79 | 3 | 0 | 0 | 0 | 0 | 0 | 1 | 0 | 4 | 0 |
| | 254/14 | 6 | 15/1 | 2 | 15/3 | 1 | 7 | 0 | 291/18 | 9 |

**Honours at Everton**
FA Cup runner-up: 1968
Football League Cup runner-up: 1976/77

# ANDY KING

*Andy King's sublime skills and enthusiasm made him an instantaneous hit.*

The 19-year old mid-fielder was snapped up by manager Billy Bingham for £35,000 after completing only 33 games with Luton Town. King's exquisite ball control, creative passing and raw passion made him popular with the fans and for an all-too-brief period his star shone brightly at Goodison. He also displayed sharp predatory skills and scored many important goals. Perhaps, none was more celebrated as his 20-yard volley against the Reds in 1978 which ended Liverpool's seven-year domination of the Merseyside showdown.

However, King's contributions became increasingly erratic and, after only 189 outings, he was sold by new manager Gordon Lee to Queen's Park Rangers for £425,000 in September 1980. Amazingly within two years, the England Under-21 star bounced back to Goodison in an exchange deal which involved Peter Eastoe moving to West Bromwich Albion.

Under the guidance of manager Howard Kendall, King started his second spell in impressive fashion until he suffered a serious knee injury. As a consequence he struggled to rediscover both his form and his flair for the unusual and was forced onto the fringes of the first-team squad as Everton emerged from the shadows.

King also had spells with Cambuur (Holland), Wolverhampton Wanderers, Luton Town and Aldershot before flirting with football management at Mansfield. Most recently he was a member of the Sunderland backroom staff.

Born: Luton, 1956
Height: 1.75 m (5 ft 9 in) Weight: 69.5 kg (10 st 13 lb)

|  | League apps | League goals | FA Cup apps | FA Cup goals | Other apps | Other goals | Europe apps | Europe goals | Total apps | Total goals |
|---|---|---|---|---|---|---|---|---|---|---|
| 1975/76 | 3 | 2 | 0 | 0 | 0 | 0 | 0 | 0 | 3 | 2 |
| 1976/77 | 36/1 | 7 | 4/1 | 0 | 9 | 5 | 0 | 0 | 49/2 | 12 |
| 1977/78 | 42 | 8 | 2 | 1 | 5 | 2 | 0 | 0 | 49 | 12 |
| 1978/79 | 40 | 12 | 1 | 0 | 3 | 0 | 3 | 4 | 47 | 16 |
| 1979/80 | 29 | 9 | 4 | 1 | 4 | 1 | 2 | 0 | 39 | 11 |
| 1982/83 | 24 | 9 | 4 | 2 | 4 | 2 | 0 | 0 | 32 | 13 |
| 1983/84 | 19/1 | 2 | 1 | 0 | 4/1 | 1 | 0 | 0 | 24/2 | 3 |
|  | 193/2 | 49 | 16/1 | 4 | 29/1 | 11 | 5 | 4 | 243/4 | 68 |

**Honours at Everton**
Milk Cup runner-up: 1983/84
Caps for England Under-21: 2

# BRIAN LABONE

*Brian Labone was renowned for combining sportsmanship with polished defensive play.*

Labone joined Everton directly from school. Even as a youngster, he was a cultured footballer possessing the essential virtues of a central defender - aerial dominance, strong tackling, astute positioning and constructive distribution. But more than his outstanding footballing skills stood him apart from his contemporaries. Labone was respected universally for his sportsmanship. His wealth of anecdotes and gentlemanly manner served to enhance the centre-half's popularity with fellow professionals and Everton fans.

Labone's reputation as a goodwill ambassador for Everton never obscured his great playing ability. The so-called 'Last of the Corinthians' was an influential member of Catterick's School of Science and two championship-winning teams. In addition, he captained Everton to their dramatic FA Cup triumph over Sheffield Wednesday in 1966. Labone was awarded 26 England caps, his first against France in 1963, and excelled in the 1970 World Cup in Mexico.

Troubled by an Achilles injury, he retired after 15 seasons at Goodison. Throughout his illustrious career and beyond, Labone has remained devoted to the royal blue faith.

Born: Liverpool, 1940
Height: 1.85 m (6 ft 1 in)  Weight: 86.3 kg (13 st 8 lb)

|  | League apps | League goals | FA Cup apps | FA Cup goals | Other apps | Other goals | Europe apps | Europe goals | Total apps | Total goals |
|---|---|---|---|---|---|---|---|---|---|---|
| 1957/58 | 4 | 0 | 0 | 0 | 0 | 0 | 0 | 0 | 4 | 0 |
| 1958/59 | 4 | 0 | 0 | 0 | 0 | 0 | 0 | 0 | 4 | 0 |
| 1959/60 | 31 | 0 | 1 | 0 | 0 | 0 | 0 | 0 | 32 | 0 |
| 1960/61 | 42 | 0 | 1 | 0 | 4 | 0 | 0 | 0 | 47 | 0 |
| 1961/62 | 41 | 0 | 3 | 0 | 0 | 0 | 0 | 0 | 44 | 0 |
| 1962/63 | 40 | 0 | 3 | 0 | 0 | 0 | 2 | 0 | 45 | 0 |
| 1963/64 | 34 | 0 | 4 | 0 | 1 | 0 | 2 | 0 | 41 | 0 |
| 1964/65 | 42 | 0 | 4 | 0 | 0 | 0 | 6 | 0 | 52 | 0 |
| 1965/66 | 37 | 2 | 8 | 0 | 0 | 0 | 3 | 0 | 48 | 2 |
| 1966/67 | 40 | 0 | 6 | 0 | 1 | 0 | 4 | 0 | 51 | 0 |
| 1967/68 | 40 | 0 | 6 | 0 | 2 | 0 | 0 | 0 | 48 | 0 |
| 1968/69 | 42 | 0 | 5 | 0 | 4 | 0 | 0 | 0 | 51 | 0 |
| 1969/70 | 34 | 0 | 1 | 0 | 4 | 0 | 0 | 0 | 39 | 0 |
| 1970/71 | 16 | 0 | 3 | 0 | 1 | 0 | 2 | 0 | 22 | 0 |
| 1971/72 | 4 | 0 | 0 | 0 | 1 | 0 | 0 | 0 | 5 | 0 |
|  | 451 | 2 | 45 | 0 | 18 | 0 | 19 | 0 | 533 | 2 |

**Honours at Everton**
Division 1 winner: 1962/63, 1969/70
FA Cup winner: 1966
FA Cup runner-up: 1968
Caps for England: 26
Caps for England Under-23: 7
Appearances for the Football League: 5

# BOB LATCHFORD

*'Big Bob' Latchford was the most expensive
and most potent striker in the 1970s.*

Cultivated by Birmingham City, Latchford was the subject of a complex part-exchange deal involving Howard Kendall and Archie Styles moving to the Midlands. The transaction was masterminded by Everton manager Billy Bingham and was valued at £350,000, a British record fee. Weighing 82.5 kg, the centre-forward was well-equipped to terrorise Division 1 defences. He was blessed with tremendous aerial power and a rasping shot, and was a natural master of converting opportunities in and around the penalty area.

Supported by the classical wing play and immaculate crosses of Dave Thomas and colleagues, Latchford was Everton's leading marksman during all of his eight seasons with the club. He reached the zenith of his career by plundering 30 goals in the 1977/78 campaign to claim a £10,000 prize from the Daily Express-Adidas. Latchford was a consistent goal-scorer and his predatory instincts were rewarded with a little less than a goal in every other game.

Although Latchford led the forward line with his own brand of bustling football, Everton's results suffered from the lack of a striking partner to take full advantage of the opportunities which he conjured up. As a consequence the rampant spearhead won few honours with Everton, far less than his talents deserved. However, he earned 12 England caps before moving to Swansea City for £125,000 in 1981. Predictably, Latchford maintained his scoring habits with the Welsh club. Towards the end of his career, he also turned out for NAC Breda (Holland), Coventry City, Lincoln City and Newport County. Latchford is youth development officer at Birmingham City.

Born: Birmingham, 1951
Height: 1.83 m (6 ft 0 in) Weight: 82.5 kg (13 st 0 lb)

| | League apps | goals | FA Cup apps | goals | Other apps | goals | Europe apps | goals | Total apps | goals |
|---|---|---|---|---|---|---|---|---|---|---|
| 1973/74 | 13 | 7 | 0 | 0 | 0 | 0 | 0 | 0 | 13 | 7 |
| 1974/75 | 36 | 17 | 3 | 1 | 2 | 1 | 0 | 0 | 41 | 19 |
| 1975/76 | 31 | 12 | 1 | 0 | 4 | 1 | 2 | 0 | 38 | 13 |
| 1976/77 | 36 | 17 | 5 | 3 | 9 | 5 | 0 | 0 | 50 | 25 |
| 1977/78 | 39 | 30 | 2 | 1 | 5 | 1 | 0 | 0 | 46 | 32 |
| 1978/79 | 36 | 11 | 1 | 0 | 3 | 6 | 4 | 3 | 44 | 20 |
| 1979/80 | 26 | 6 | 5/1 | 5 | 2 | 2 | 0/1 | 0 | 33/2 | 13 |
| 1980/81 | 18/1 | 6 | 0 | 0 | 3 | 3 | 0 | 0 | 21/1 | 9 |
| | 235/1 | 106 | 17/1 | 10 | 28 | 19 | 6/1 | 3 | 286/3 | 138 |

**Honours at Everton**
Football League Cup runner-up: 1976/77
Caps for England: 12
Caps for England Under-23: 4
Appearances for the Football League: 1

# ALEX LATTA

*Alex Latta was famed for his dashing displays and goal-scoring exploits.*

Latta sharpened his skills with Dumbarton Athletic before teaming up with the Toffees in 1889. The 22-year old flankman was the first professional import from the Scottish town which proved to be a fertile recruiting ground for Everton before the turn of the century. During his time on Merseyside, Latta was joined by several other quality players from the Dumbarton area including Richard Boyle, John Bell, John Robertson and Jack Taylor.

Latta was an accomplished outside-right and had established a reputation in Scotland for exciting wing-play. He had been awarded two caps by his country, his first in 1885. Although Latta was big for a Victorian winger at 83.5 kg, his lightning acceleration, intricate dribbling and goal-scoring instincts were well-respected by opponents. He also possessed a powerful shot and found the target 70 times during his seven seasons with the club. Alongside Fred Geary and Alex Brady, Latta was an invaluable member of the Everton team to capture the League championship in 1890/91. He also played in the 1893 FA Cup final in which the Toffees were defeated by Wolverhampton Wanderers at Fallowfield.

Latta was one of the outstanding personalities of early Merseyside football and was something of a maverick both on and off the pitch. As a result, he was often at odds with Everton's directors and returned to Anfield Road in 1896. However, there is no record of him having played first-team football for Liverpool.

Born: Dumbarton, 1867
Height: 1.75 m (5 ft 9 in) Weight: 83.5 kg (13 st 2 lb)

|  | League apps | League goals | FA Cup apps | FA Cup goals | Total apps | Total goals |
|---|---|---|---|---|---|---|
| 1889/90 | 19 | 9 | 2 | 0 | 21 | 9 |
| 1890/91 | 10 | 4 | 1 | 0 | 11 | 4 |
| 1891/92 | 25 | 17 | 1 | 0 | 26 | 17 |
| 1892/93 | 28 | 18 | 7 | 1 | 35 | 19 |
| 1893/94 | 29 | 9 | 1 | 0 | 30 | 9 |
| 1894/95 | 20 | 11 | 0 | 0 | 20 | 11 |
| 1895/96 | 5 | 1 | 0 | 0 | 5 | 1 |
|  | 136 | 69 | 12 | 1 | 148 | 70 |

**Honours at Everton**
League winner: 1890/91
League runner-up: 1889/90, 1894/95
FA Cup (English Cup) runner-up: 1893

# TOMMY LAWTON

*Tommy Lawton was a majestic footballer,*
*one of the greatest-ever centre-forwards.*

Arguably a better all-round footballer than his predecessor, Lawton was unquestionably head and shoulders above his contemporaries and was the only centre-forward capable of filling Dixie Dean's boots. As a schoolboy prodigy, Lawton scored an unparalleled 570 goals in three seasons. He graduated through the amateur ranks of Hayes Athletic and Rossendale United to senior football with Burnley, scoring freely at all levels. Lawton signed professional forms with the Turf Moor-club in October 1936, and after a series of clandestine negotiations, was acquired by Everton for £6,500 in early-1937. The deal also required the club to add James Riley, a relative of the player, to its ground staff. The 17-year old rookie played at inside-forward alongside Dean before succeeding the Goodison legend at the centre of the attack. Lawton quickly reinforced his reputation. The outstanding marksman was brilliant on the ground and lethal in the air, both in power and direction.

Lawton topped the Football League goal-scorers' list in 1937/38 and, amid the threats of gas masks and air-raid shelters, netted 34 goals in 38 League outings in the 1938/39 championship crusade. Overall, he averaged 0.737 goals per game. Lawton represented the Football League on two occasions, scoring four goals against the Irish League in 1938, and earned eight England caps in 1939. Indisputably, the six years of hostilities denied the star centre-forward his finest days. Notwithstanding, he continued to turn out for Everton in regional football and amassed 109 goals in 149 outings. He also played for Aldershot, Tranmere Rovers and Morton in war-time fixtures.

Immediately after the resumption of peace-time football, the Everton and England star rocked Goodison Park by submitting a transfer request. Lawton had been the corner-stone of Everton's post-war ambitions, but reluctantly was allowed to leave the club on compassionate grounds. He joined Chelsea for £11,500 in 1945 and played for Notts County, Brentford and Arsenal before turning his hand to management at Kettering Town and Notts County.

Born: Bolton, 1919
Height: 1.80 m (5 ft 11 in) Weight: 76.3 kg (12 st 0 lb)

|  | League | | FA Cup | | Other | | Total | |
|---|---|---|---|---|---|---|---|---|
|  | apps | goals | apps | goals | apps | goals | apps | goals |
| 1936/37 | 10 | 3 | 1 | 1 | 0 | 0 | 11 | 4 |
| 1937/38 | 39 | 28 | 2 | 0 | 3 | 2 | 44 | 30 |
| 1938/39 | 38 | 34 | 5 | 4 | 0 | 0 | 44 | 39 |
|  | 87 | 65 | 8 | 5 | 3 | 2 | 99 | 73 |

**Honours at Everton**
Division 1 winner: 1938/39
Caps for England: 8
War-time internationals: 18
Appearances for the Football League: 2

# MIKE LYONS

*Mike Lyons was a versatile player and a devoted Evertonian.*

The Croxteth apprentice graduated through Everton's nursery system to make his senior debut as a striker in 1971. Lyons compensated for his modest footballing skills with awesome athleticism. His greatest assets were his physical strength and unflagging appetite for honest endeavour. He was prepared to run tirelessly all over the pitch for Everton and never shirked a challenge.

Lyons notched up over 450 first-team appearances during his Goodison career and threw his royal blue heart and soul into every contest. As a raw youngster, he alternated between mid-field and attack before confounding his critics by developing into a spirited club captain and an authoritative central defender renowned for his powerful tackling. Although Lyons seemed to understand the devotion of the Goodison fans far better than any player of his generation, Everton failed to win any major trophies under his leadership. He was selected by England Under-23 and England 'B', but such was his luck - the 'B' international game against Czechoslovakia in 1978 was abandoned due to torrential rain.

In the twilight of his career, the proud blue-blood moved to Sheffield Wednesday. He also enjoyed a spell as player-manager at Grimsby Town before joining the Bellefield staff as reserve-team coach in 1987. Lyons subsequently coached Huddersfield Town and the Brunei national team.

Born: Liverpool, 1951
Height: 1.83 m (6 ft 0 in) Weight: 78.1 kg (12 st 4 lb)

|  | League apps | League goals | FA Cup apps | FA Cup goals | Other apps | Other goals | Europe apps | Europe goals | Total apps | Total goals |
|---|---|---|---|---|---|---|---|---|---|---|
| 1970/71 | 1/1 | 1 | 0 | 0 | 0 | 0 | 0 | 0 | 1/1 | 1 |
| 1971/72 | 20/4 | 3 | 4 | 0 | 0 | 0 | 0 | 0 | 24/4 | 3 |
| 1972/73 | 19/6 | 2 | 0 | 0 | 1 | 0 | 0 | 0 | 20/6 | 2 |
| 1973/74 | 37/4 | 9 | 3 | 0 | 3 | 0 | 0 | 0 | 43/4 | 9 |
| 1974/75 | 36/2 | 8 | 4 | 3 | 2 | 0 | 0 | 0 | 42/2 | 11 |
| 1975/76 | 42 | 5 | 1 | 0 | 5 | 1 | 2 | 0 | 50 | 6 |
| 1976/77 | 39/1 | 4 | 7 | 1 | 9 | 2 | 0 | 0 | 55/1 | 7 |
| 1977/78 | 42 | 5 | 2 | 1 | 5 | 2 | 0 | 0 | 49 | 8 |
| 1978/79 | 37 | 6 | 1 | 0 | 2 | 0 | 3 | 0 | 43 | 6 |
| 1979/80 | 35/3 | 0 | 6 | 0 | 5 | 0 | 2 | 0 | 48/3 | 0 |
| 1980/81 | 30/3 | 2 | 0/1 | 1 | 0 | 0 | 0 | 0 | 30/4 | 3 |
| 1981/82 | 26/1 | 3 | 1 | 0 | 4 | 0 | 0 | 0 | 31/1 | 3 |
|  | 364/25 | 48 | 29/1 | 6 | 36 | 5 | 7 | 0 | 436/26 | 59 |

**Honours at Everton**
Football League Cup runner-up: 1976/77
Caps for England Under-23: 5
Caps for England 'B': 1

# Mr George Mahon

*George Mahon steered the club from Anfield to more palatial accommodation.*

Mahon had been the choir-master at St Domingo Congregational Church and was a keen supporter of Everton. Along with James Baxter, he joined the management committee of the club in 1889 and rose to prominence shortly after Everton had carried off the Football League championship in 1890/91. Drawing on his business acumen gained as the head of a firm of accountants in North John Street, Mahon was well-respected by the club members.

Accordingly, when the affairs of the club were thrown into turmoil in early 1892, Mahon led the vigorous objections of several members to the club being headquartered at the Sandon Hotel and to the rent increases proposed by John Houlding, their Anfield landlord. Everton's playing success had encouraged Houlding to double the annual rent. Although the landlord responded to these objections by serving the club with a notice to quit, Mahon had already negotiated an option on a site on the northern side of Stanley Park. As a result, the club vacated Anfield for Mere Green Field, Walton and within months had invested £3,500 in constructing the most advanced football stadium in Europe. Goodison Park was opened by Lord Kinnaird in August 1892 and Mahon arranged for the purchase of the land three years later.

Supported by committee members such as Dr JC Baxter and WR Clayton, Mahon converted the club into a limited liability company. He established the company structure, financing arrangements and administrative procedures and served as chairman until tendering his resignation *"owing to acute administrative differences"* along with four other directors in 1895. Subsequently, Mahon was re-instated as a director and specialised in managing the financial matters of the club for several seasons before his premature death in 1908.

Born: Liverpool, circa 1855
**Everton director/chairman:** 19 years

**Everton record during term**
League: 304 wins, 111 draws, 229 defeats

**Everton honours during term**
League champions: 1890/91
League runners-up: 1889/90
Division 1 runners-up: 1894/95, 1901/02, 1904/05
FA Cup (English Cup) winners: 1906
FA Cup (English Cup) runners-up: 1893, 1897, 1907

# HARRY MAKEPEACE

*Harry Makepeace was a superlative*
*sportsman who advanced football's image.*

Born in Middlesbrough but raised in Liverpool, Makepeace kicked off his career with Everton in 1902. The wing-half did not boast a commanding stature but matured into a key member of several successful Everton teams. His fierce tackling, neat passing and astute football brain were equally effective at right-half or left-half. But perhaps more than anything, the model professional was renowned for his exemplary behaviour. Makepeace participated in 336 games with Everton including consecutive English Cup finals in 1906 and 1907. After near-misses in 1904/05 and 1908/09, his deeds on the pitch were rewarded with a League championship medal in 1914/15. In addition, he earned four England caps.

Immediately after World War I, Makepeace was appointed coach at Everton and concentrated on his cricketing exploits at Lancashire County CC. He was selected to play in four Test matches. As a result he shared with Jack Sharp, his Everton and Lancashire colleague, the distinction of representing England at both football and cricket. Between 1906-1930, Makepeace played 499 first-class matches and 778 innings. He amassed 25,745 runs including 43 centuries, took 42 wickets and held 194 catches. As an opening batsman, Makepeace scored 117 against Australia at Melbourne in 1921 and became the oldest player to score a maiden Test century. At the end of his cricketing career, Makepeace served Lancashire for another 20 years as coach.

Born: Middlesbrough, 1881
Height: 1.70 m (5 ft 7 in)  Weight: 63.6 kg (10 st 0 lb)

|  | League apps | League goals | FA Cup apps | FA Cup goals | Total apps | Total goals |
|---|---|---|---|---|---|---|
| 1902/03 | 3 | 0 | 1 | 0 | 4 | 0 |
| 1904/05 | 19 | 5 | 6 | 2 | 25 | 7 |
| 1905/06 | 27 | 2 | 6 | 2 | 33 | 4 |
| 1906/07 | 23 | 0 | 8 | 0 | 31 | 0 |
| 1907/08 | 31 | 2 | 7 | 0 | 38 | 2 |
| 1908/09 | 33 | 0 | 2 | 0 | 35 | 0 |
| 1909/10 | 32 | 4 | 7 | 2 | 39 | 6 |
| 1910/11 | 33 | 1 | 3 | 0 | 36 | 1 |
| 1911/12 | 34 | 1 | 5 | 1 | 39 | 2 |
| 1912/13 | 10 | 0 | 1 | 0 | 11 | 0 |
| 1913/14 | 16 | 0 | 1 | 0 | 17 | 0 |
| 1914/15 | 23 | 1 | 5 | 0 | 28 | 1 |
|  | 284 | 16 | 52 | 7 | 336 | 23 |

**Honours at Everton**
Division 1 winner: 1914/15
Division 1 runner-up: 1904/05, 1908/09
FA Cup (English Cup) winner: 1906
FA Cup (English Cup) runner-up: 1907
Caps for England: 4
Appearances for the Football League: 5

# JOE MERCER

*Joe Mercer was one of Goodison's favourite sons and one of England's all-time greats.*

After spells with Ellesmere Port Town, Shell Mex and Elton Green, Mercer came to the attention of Everton in 1931. He played in the Central League team as a 15-year old and was baptised in the top flight immediately after turning professional. By 1938, Mercer had gained his first England cap.

The world-class wing-half possessed a superb football brain and displayed intelligence, vision and guile in all aspects of his game. His precise passing and astute positional play made the game look deceptively easy. Capitalising on his ability to efficiently convert defence into attack, Mercer became a cornerstone of Goodison's first School of Science and played an inspirational role in the 1938/39 championship triumph. Sadly like most of his team-mates, his career was impacted by World War II. Nevertheless, Sergeant Major Mercer of the Army Physical Training Corps was promoted to captain of England and made 26 appearances in war-time and victory internationals. He also represented the Football League against the Scottish League in 1941 in an RAF benefit match. Unfortunately, Mercer became disenchanted with Everton and was sold to Arsenal for £7,000 in late 1946.

After leaving Everton, Mercer continued to live on Merseyside and train at Anfield. He led the Gunners to two League championships and two FA Cup finals, and was also voted FWA 'Footballer of the Year' in 1950s before moving into football management with Sheffield United, Aston Villa, Manchester City and Coventry City. Mercer was awarded the OBE in 1976 and temporarily took charge of the England national team. Although he enjoyed significant success as a player and a manager, few doubted that Mercer was proud of the royal blue blood in his veins.

Born: Ellesmere Port, 1914
Height: 1.75 m (5 ft 9 in)  Weight: 70.0 kg (11 st 0 lb)

|  | League | | FA Cup | | Others | | Total | |
|---|---|---|---|---|---|---|---|---|
|  | apps | goals | apps | goals | apps | goals | apps | goals |
| 1932/33 | 1 | 0 | 0 | 0 | 0 | 0 | 1 | 0 |
| 1934/35 | 8 | 0 | 0 | 0 | 0 | 0 | 8 | 0 |
| 1935/36 | 33 | 1 | 1 | 0 | 0 | 0 | 34 | 1 |
| 1936/37 | 39 | 0 | 4 | 0 | 0 | 0 | 43 | 0 |
| 1937/38 | 36 | 0 | 2 | 0 | 3 | 0 | 41 | 0 |
| 1938/39 | 41 | 0 | 5 | 0 | 1 | 0 | 47 | 0 |
| 1945/46 | 0 | 0 | 2 | 1 | 0 | 0 | 2 | 1 |
| 1946/47 | 12 | 0 | 0 | 0 | 0 | 0 | 12 | 0 |
|  | 170 | 1 | 14 | 1 | 4 | 0 | 188 | 2 |

**Honours at Everton**
Division 1 winner: 1938/39
Caps for England: 5
Victory internationals: 2
War-time internationals: 24
War-time appearances for the Football League: 1

# ALF MILWARD

*Alf Milward was one of the pioneering*
*professionals of the last century.*

Milward arrived from Great Marlow, one of the pioneering teams of Victorian football, during the inaugural season of the Football League and quickly established himself as the first choice outside-left at Everton. He had a professional appetite for hard work as well as a never-say-die attitude and developed into one of the most feared forwards of his generation. His whippet-like pace left defenders trailing in his wake and his distinguished left-wing partnership with Edgar Chadwick was devastating.

Milward was ever-present during Everton's first championship season and also contributed 12 goals. Despite his impressive strike-rate, success in the English Cup final eluded him. He collected runners-up medals for his frustrating close-shaves with Everton in 1893 and 1897 and with Southampton in 1902. He was awarded four international caps and, alongside team-mates Edgar Chadwick, Fred Geary and Johnny Holt, turned out for England against Scotland in 1891. Also he was selected to represent the Football League in 1896.

Milward joined ill-fated New Brighton Tower of Division 2 in 1897 and later moved on to Southampton, where he won a Southern League championship medal. He concluded his career with New Brompton before retiring in 1903.

Born: Marlow, 1870
Height: 1.73 m (5 ft 8 in) Weight: 76.3 kg (12 st 0 lb)

|  | League apps | League goals | FA Cup apps | FA Cup goals | Total apps | Total goals |
|---|---|---|---|---|---|---|
| 1888/89 | 6 | 2 | 0 | 0 | 6 | 2 |
| 1889/90 | 22 | 10 | 2 | 4 | 24 | 14 |
| 1890/91 | 22 | 12 | 1 | 0 | 23 | 12 |
| 1891/92 | 26 | 6 | 1 | 0 | 27 | 6 |
| 1892/93 | 27 | 11 | 7 | 2 | 34 | 13 |
| 1893/94 | 24 | 8 | 1 | 0 | 25 | 8 |
| 1894/95 | 18 | 10 | 3 | 0 | 21 | 10 |
| 1895/96 | 29 | 17 | 3 | 2 | 32 | 19 |
| 1896/97 | 27 | 9 | 5 | 3 | 32 | 12 |
| | 201 | 85 | 23 | 11 | 224 | 96 |

**Honours at Everton**
League winner: 1890/91
League runner-up: 1889/90
Division 1 runner-up: 1894/95
FA Cup (English Cup) runner-up: 1893, 1897
Caps for England: 4
Appearances for the Football League: 1

# SIR JOHN MOORES

*John Moores was a visionary businessman
and the club's greatest benefactor.*

Moores, the son of a bricklayer, made his fortune through a portfolio of companies involved in football pools, department stores and mail-order catalogues and was reputed to be one of the richest men in Europe. He was a keen football fan and acquired his first shares in Everton during the club's darkest hours in Division 2. Moores continued to increase his share-holding throughout the 1950s, gradually gaining a controlling interest in the club.

The self-made billionaire was indifferent to the luxuries that money could buy but, in his role as club benefactor, advanced interest-free funds for the rebuilding of the team. Consequently Everton manager Johnny Carey, as well as his successor Harry Catterick, was equipped to target the best talent available in the transfer market and invested about £100,000 in acquiring star players such as Tommy Ring, Roy Vernon, Jimmy Gabriel and Micky Lill during the 1959/60 season. Predictably, Everton were labelled the 'Bank of England Club' and the 'Merseyside Millionaires'. Moores was elected club chairman in 1960 and set about applying his immense commercial expertise to strengthen the financial health of Everton. He promised to leave no stone unturned in providing the success-starved fans with the best facilities and a team equal to the great Everton sides of the past. Moores also worked diligently at enhancing operations behind the scenes as well as the accommodation at Goodison Park and the training facilities at Bellefield.

The Everton chairman was a man of high standards. Honesty and integrity were his watchwords and he applied the club's motto both on and off the field. Under his stewardship, the Toffees captured two League titles and the FA Cup. Moores took a back-seat in 1965 but, after a spate of indifferent results, returned as chairman at the age of 76 to steer the club through the 1972/73 season. The life-long Evertonian continued to attend matches at Goodison Park into his nineties.

Moores donated millions to charity and was knighted in 1980. He died in 1993.

Born: Eccles, 1896
**Everton director/chairman:** 17 years

**Everton record during term**
League: 307 wins, 201 draws, 206 defeats

**Everton honours during term**
Division 1 champions: 1962/63, 1969/70
FA Cup winners: 1966
FA Cup runners-up: 1968

# JOHNNY MORRISSEY

*Johnny Morrissey needed his muscle-man's physique to carry his abundance of skills.*

Discovered by Liverpool, Morrissey transferred his loyalties to Everton in 1962. The £10,000 deal was one of Everton manager Harry Catterick's most inspirational transactions, much to the displeasure of Anfield boss Bill Shankly.

Morrissey was one of the most under-rated players in the country and his muscular appearance masked his tremendous football skills. He was blessed with immaculate ball control technique and loved to run at defenders. Equally as daunting, the stocky left-winger was not someone to be tangled with - even during training sessions. Some adversaries claimed that Morrissey was strong in the tackle, whereas others reflected that he was simply as hard as nails.

Morrissey's powerful shooting contributed several vital goals throughout his decade at Everton. After missing out on the 1966 FA Cup victory, he reached the pinnacle of his career in the late 1960s when he complemented the mid-field triumvirate of Kendall, Harvey & Ball. In fact, during the 1969/70 championship campaign there was no finer winger in the British game. Morrissey was selected to represent the Football League in 1969, but other international honours eluded him. He moved to Oldham Athletic in 1972 and retired shortly afterwards.

Born: Liverpool, 1940
Height: 1.70 m (5 ft 7 in)  Weight: 74.5 kg (11 st 10 lb)

| | League apps | goals | FA Cup apps | goals | Other apps | goals | Europe apps | goals | Total apps | goals |
|---|---|---|---|---|---|---|---|---|---|---|
| 1962/63 | 28 | 7 | 3 | 1 | 0 | 0 | 2 | 0 | 33 | 8 |
| 1963/64 | 7 | 1 | 0 | 0 | 0 | 0 | 0 | 0 | 7 | 1 |
| 1964/65 | 25 | 5 | 4 | 0 | 0 | 0 | 4 | 1 | 33 | 6 |
| 1965/66 | 10/1 | 2 | 1 | 0 | 0 | 0 | 3 | 0 | 14/1 | 2 |
| 1966/67 | 31 | 6 | 6 | 0 | 0 | 0 | 3 | 1 | 40 | 7 |
| 1967/68 | 26 | 3 | 5 | 2 | 1 | 0 | 0 | 0 | 32 | 5 |
| 1968/69 | 40 | 4 | 5 | 0 | 4 | 1 | 0 | 0 | 49 | 5 |
| 1969/70 | 41 | 9 | 1 | 0 | 3 | 0 | 0 | 0 | 45 | 9 |
| 1970/71 | 34 | 6 | 4 | 0 | 0 | 0 | 6 | 1 | 44 | 7 |
| 1971/72 | 15/1 | 0 | 0 | 0 | 0 | 0 | 0 | 0 | 15/1 | 0 |
| | 257/2 | 43 | 29 | 3 | 8 | 1 | 18 | 3 | 312/2 | 50 |

**Honours at Everton**
Division 1 winner: 1962/63, 1969/70
FA Cup runner-up: 1968
Appearances for the Football League: 1

# ALEX PARKER

*Alex Parker was a polished defender
renowned for his sliding tackles.*

A graduate of Kello Rovers, the 23-year old full-back arrived at Goodison with winger
Eddie O'Hara from Falkirk for a joint fee of £25,500.  Parker was valued at £18,000.
His debut was delayed by his National Service commitments with the Royal Scots
Fusiliers in Cyprus.  But after a short period of acclimatisation at Everton, his form was
sensational.  The unruffled right-back was an impressive addition to the playing staff
with his astute positioning and beautifully weighted crosses.  He liked to make
adventurous forays in support of his forwards but, more than anything, was acclaimed
for perfecting the sliding tackle technique.  His impeccably timed tackles and
respectable turn of speed gave him tremendous powers of recovery.

The established Scotland international was an important member of Everton's 1962/63
championship team.  With the recruitment of England left-back Ray Wilson in 1964,
the club had envisioned that Parker and Wilson would develop into a world-class
partnership.  Regrettably they were restricted to playing only two games together
before Parker was side-lined by a serious injury.  Parker never fully recovered and
moved to Southport in 1965.  Subsequently, he tasted football management with
Ballymena United, Drumcondra and Southport.

Mystifyingly, Parker's transfer to Everton essentially ended his international career.
In total he clocked up 15 appearances for Scotland, his first at age 19, but was
selected only once during his Goodison career - against Paraguay in 1958.

Born:  Irvine, 1935
Height:  1.72 m (5 ft 8 in)  Weight:  75.8 kg (11 st 13 lb)

|  | League | | FA Cup | | Other | | Europe | | Total | |
| --- | apps | goals | apps | goals | apps | goals | apps | goals | apps | goals |
| 1958/59 | 26 | 1 | 4 | 0 | 0 | 0 | 0 | 0 | 30 | 1 |
| 1959/60 | 38 | 2 | 1 | 0 | 0 | 0 | 0 | 0 | 39 | 2 |
| 1960/61 | 41 | 0 | 1 | 0 | 5 | 0 | 0 | 0 | 47 | 0 |
| 1961/62 | 31 | 0 | 3 | 0 | 0 | 0 | 0 | 0 | 34 | 0 |
| 1962/63 | 33 | 2 | 3 | 0 | 0 | 0 | 2 | 0 | 38 | 2 |
| 1963/64 | 17 | 0 | 0 | 0 | 1 | 0 | 2 | 0 | 20 | 0 |
| 1964/65 | 12 | 0 | 0 | 0 | 0 | 0 | 0 | 0 | 12 | 0 |
|  | 198 | 5 | 12 | 0 | 6 | 0 | 4 | 0 | 220 | 5 |

**Honours at Everton**
Division 1 winner:  1962/63
Caps for Scotland:  1

# BOBBY PARKER

*Bobby Parker was the leading marksman
of the Great War era.*

Purchased from Glasgow Rangers for £1,500 in 1913, Parker made an immediate impact at Everton by scoring 10 times in his first 12 League games. Although his aerial prowess was somewhat limited, few fans doubted that Everton had acquired a centre-forward of proven quality with a powerful shot in both feet.

Although Parker was the victim of close marking, he was surprisingly tough to knock off the ball. Most defences were incapable of stifling his talents and his goal-scoring feats were impressive, given that they were established under the old off-side law which required three opponents goal-side of the attacker. Parker tended to grab goals in clusters of twos and threes. He tormented opposing defences throughout the 1914/15 campaign and found the target 35 times in 36 Division 1 games. In fact, only spells of indifferent form and injury towards the end of the season prevented him from equalling Bertie Freeman's record of 37 goals in 38 League games. Nevertheless his partnership with inside-left Joe Clennell ensured that the Toffees secured the Division 1 crown.

With Parker leading the attack, Everton had looked set to reach new heights before World War I was declared but were restricted to participating in regional football between 1915/16-1918/19. Like many members of the 1914/15 championship side, Parker's career was severely impacted by the outbreak of hostilities. However, with the resumption of peace-time football, he continued to score regularly. Despite averaging 0.775 goals per game throughout his stay at Goodison, Parker received no international honours. Possibly the Scotland selectors ignored his claims because he played most of his football south of the border. Parker moved to Nottingham Forest in 1921.

Born: Possil Park, Glasgow 1891
Height: 1.67 m (5 ft 6 in) Weight: 71.3 kg (11 st 3 lb)

|  | League apps | League goals | FA Cup apps | FA Cup goals | Total apps | Total goals |
|---|---|---|---|---|---|---|
| 1913/14 | 24 | 17 | 1 | 0 | 25 | 17 |
| 1914/15 | 35 | 36 | 5 | 2 | 40 | 38 |
| 1919/20 | 8 | 4 | 0 | 0 | 8 | 4 |
| 1920/21 | 17 | 11 | 2 | 1 | 19 | 12 |
|  | 84 | 68 | 8 | 3 | 92 | 71 |

**Honours at Everton**
Division 1 winner: 1914/15

# JOHN WILLIE PARKER

*John Willie Parker scored the vital goals*
*which returned the club to the top flight.*

Parker was recruited as an enthusiastic amateur from the anonymity of St Lawrence CYMS in 1948. He was a clinical finisher, blessed with natural goal-scoring instincts, and thrived on converting the goal-scoring opportunities created by centre-forward Dave Hickson. Parker's talents were best characterised by his two strikes at Oldham Athletic in the 1953/54 season which enabled Everton to escape the shackles of Division 2.

Although the stylish inside-left appeared somewhat fragile, he possessed a stinging shot. Parker dovetailed effectively with Hickson and established a formidable spearhead with his rumbustious striking-partner. In tandem, they were endowed with the essential requirements of courage, mobility, firepower and sharpness around the penalty area and produced 56 League goals to return Everton to Division 1.

The Everton shooting-star played most of his football in Division 2 and was the club's leading marksman in all three of their seasons in the lower League. For a short time, his marksmanship flourished against top flight defences but, with the transfer of Hickson to Aston Villa in 1955, Parker struggled to carry the responsibilities of the Everton front-line and his star status diminished.

Parker averaged a goal in every other game with Everton before reverting to second division football with Bury in 1956.

Born: Birkenhead, 1925
Height: 1.78 m (5 ft 10 in)  Weight: 70.8 kg (11 st 2 lb)

|  | League | | FA Cup | | Total | |
|---|---|---|---|---|---|---|
|  | apps | goals | apps | goals | apps | goals |
| 1950/51 | 7 | 0 | 0 | 0 | 7 | 0 |
| 1951/52 | 36 | 15 | 2 | 1 | 38 | 16 |
| 1952/53 | 32 | 13 | 4 | 4 | 36 | 17 |
| 1953/54 | 38 | 31 | 3 | 2 | 41 | 33 |
| 1954/55 | 34 | 19 | 0 | 0 | 34 | 19 |
| 1955/56 | 20 | 4 | 0 | 0 | 20 | 4 |
|  | 167 | 82 | 9 | 7 | 176 | 89 |

**Honours at Everton**
Division 2 runner-up: 1953/54

# KEVIN RATCLIFFE

*Kevin Ratcliffe was the most successful captain in Everton's history.*

As an apprentice professional, Ratcliffe demonstrated a tremendous willingness to learn his trade and made his first-team debut in 1980. Frustrated at being played out of position, he was rumoured to be on the verge of leaving the club before manager Howard Kendall offered him the chance to replace Billy Wright at centre-half. Ratcliffe never looked back and, shortly afterwards, claimed the captaincy of his club and country.

The commanding pivot was arguably the quickest defender of his generation and with help from Derek Mountfield and Neville Southall galvanised the Everton defence. He led the pursuit for silverware throughout the glory days of the mid-1980s and skippered the Toffees to two Division 1 championships as well as triumphs in the FA Cup and the European Cup-Winners' Cup. Capped 58 times by Wales, Ratcliffe concluded his playing career with brief spells at Dundee, Cardiff City, Nottingham Forest, Derby County and Chester City and embarked on his management career with Chester and Shrewsbury Town.

Born: Mancot, Flintshire, 1960
Height: 1.80 m (5 ft 11 in)   Weight: 79.0 kg (12 st 6 lb)

| | League apps | League goals | FA Cup apps | FA Cup goals | Other apps | Other goals | Europe apps | Europe goals | Total apps | Total goals |
|---|---|---|---|---|---|---|---|---|---|---|
| 1979/80 | 2 | 0 | 1 | 0 | 0 | 0 | 0 | 0 | 3 | 0 |
| 1980/81 | 20/1 | 0 | 5 | 0 | 2 | 0 | 0 | 0 | 27/1 | 0 |
| 1981/82 | 25 | 0 | 1 | 0 | 1 | 0 | 0 | 0 | 27 | 0 |
| 1982/83 | 29 | 1 | 5 | 0 | 3 | 0 | 0 | 0 | 37 | 1 |
| 1983/84 | 38 | 0 | 8 | 0 | 11 | 0 | 0 | 0 | 57 | 0 |
| 1984/85 | 40 | 0 | 7 | 0 | 5 | 0 | 9 | 0 | 61 | 0 |
| 1985/86 | 39 | 1 | 5 | 0 | 12 | 0 | 0 | 0 | 56 | 1 |
| 1986/87 | 42 | 0 | 3 | 0 | 7 | 0 | 0 | 0 | 52 | 0 |
| 1987/88 | 24 | 0 | 1 | 0 | 6 | 0 | 0 | 0 | 31 | 0 |
| 1988/89 | 30 | 0 | 8 | 0 | 8 | 0 | 0 | 0 | 46 | 0 |
| 1989/90 | 24 | 0 | 7 | 0 | 2 | 0 | 0 | 0 | 33 | 0 |
| 1990/91 | 35/1 | 0 | 6 | 0 | 8/1 | 0 | 0 | 0 | 49/2 | 0 |
| 1991/92 | 8/1 | 0 | 0 | 0 | 2/1 | 0 | 0 | 0 | 10/2 | 0 |
| | 356/3 | 2 | 57 | 0 | 67/2 | 0 | 9 | 0 | 489/5 | 2 |

**Honours at Everton**
Division 1 winner: 1984/85, 1986/87
Division 1 runner-up: 1985/86
European Cup-Winners' Cup winner: 1985
FA Cup winner: 1984
FA Cup runner-up: 1985, 1986, 1989
Milk Cup runner-up: 1983/84
Simod Cup runner-up: 1988/89
Zenith Data Systems Cup runner-up: 1990/91
Screen Sport Super Cup runner-up: 1985/86
Caps for Wales: 58
Caps for Wales Under-21: 2

# PETER REID

*Peter Reid was a bargain buy and was instrumental in the successes of the 1980s.*

Everton picked up Reid for £60,000 from Bolton Wanderers in 1982. The transaction was a bargain, given that the club had agreed a fee of ten times that amount less than three seasons earlier. However during that period, the mid-fielder's progress had been disrupted by a series of career-threatening injuries including a broken kneecap, a fractured leg and a cartilage operation. Fortunately, his cornucopia of skills remained undamaged.

Reid, a tenacious tackler and an immaculate passer of the ball, linked up admirably with Paul Bracewell to become a significant driving force behind the most successful period in the club's history. His never-say-die attitude inspired his colleagues and also captured the admiration of the Goodison fans in a manner granted to only a select band of players down the years. As a result of his growl and snap, the Toffees won an abundance of trophies. Two Division 1 titles, the FA Cup and the club's first European trophy bear testament to his unflagging commitment to the royal blue cause.

He was awarded 13 England caps, his first as a substitute against Mexico in 1985, and became the first Everton player to be voted PFA 'Player of the Year'. Subsequently, Reid was appointed player-coach at Everton but parted company with the club in 1989 when he joined Queen's Park Rangers on a free transfer. He teamed up again with Howard Kendall as player-coach at Manchester City and was later elevated to player-manager. After leaving Maine Road, Reid played a few games with Southampton, Notts County and Bury before continuing in football management with Sunderland.

Born: Huyton, 1956
Height: 1.67 m (5 ft 6 in)  Weight: 71.3 kg (11 st 3 lb)

| | League apps | goals | FA Cup apps | goals | Other apps | goals | Europe apps | goals | Total apps | goals |
|---|---|---|---|---|---|---|---|---|---|---|
| 1982/83 | 7 | 0 | 3 | 0 | 0 | 0 | 0 | 0 | 10 | 0 |
| 1983/84 | 34/1 | 2 | 8 | 1 | 9/1 | 1 | 0 | 0 | 51/2 | 4 |
| 1984/85 | 36 | 2 | 7 | 1 | 5 | 0 | 9 | 1 | 57 | 4 |
| 1985/86 | 15 | 1 | 5 | 0 | 2 | 0 | 0 | 0 | 22 | 1 |
| 1986/87 | 15/1 | 1 | 2 | 0 | 0 | 0 | 0 | 0 | 17/1 | 1 |
| 1987/88 | 32 | 1 | 8 | 1 | 8 | 0 | 0 | 0 | 48 | 2 |
| 1988/89 | 16/2 | 1 | 2 | 0 | 6/1 | 0 | 0 | 0 | 24/3 | 1 |
| | 155/4 | 8 | 35 | 3 | 30/2 | 1 | 9 | 1 | 229/6 | 13 |

### Honours at Everton
Division 1 winner: 1984/85, 1986/87
Division 1 runner-up: 1985/86
European Cup-Winners' Cup winner: 1985
FA Cup winner: 1984
FA Cup runner-up: 1985, 1986
Milk Cup runner-up: 1983/84
Caps for England: 13

# JOE ROYLE

*Joe Royle became Everton's youngest star
at the tender age of 16 years 282 days.*

Royle made his debut for the Toffees under somewhat controversial circumstances at Blackpool in 1966. Harry Catterick had picked the 16-year old centre-forward at the expense of Goodison idol Alex Young and some Everton supporters demonstrated their disapproval by man-handling the manager after the game.

Standing 1.83 m and 83.5 kg, the young striker from Norris Green blossomed into an accomplished leader of the Everton attack. Royle used his massive physique to great effect and developed into a tremendous header of the ball, scoring 23 goals during the 1969/70 championship drive. A cruel spate of back and knee injuries affected the remainder of his Goodison career and Royle earned no more silverware with the Toffees before leaving for Manchester City in 1975. He was awarded two England caps during his time at Everton, his first against Malta in 1971.

After stints with Bristol City and Norwich City, he moved into football management and steered Oldham Athletic into Division 1. The Goodison old-boy grasped the poisoned royal blue chalice after the termination of Mike Walker's contract in 1994. During Royle's fleeting spell at the helm, the club spent over £30 million on new playing staff and won the FA Cup in 1995. But sadly further success eluded them. Royle resigned in 1997 and subsequently took over the reigns at Maine Road.

Born: Liverpool, 1949
Height: 1.83 m (6 ft 0 in)  Weight: 83.5 kg (13 st 2 lb)

| | League apps | League goals | FA Cup apps | FA Cup goals | Other apps | Other goals | Europe apps | Europe goals | Total apps | Total goals |
|---|---|---|---|---|---|---|---|---|---|---|
| 1965/66 | 2 | 0 | 0 | 0 | 0 | 0 | 0 | 0 | 2 | 0 |
| 1966/67 | 4 | 3 | 0 | 0 | 0 | 0 | 0 | 0 | 4 | 3 |
| 1967/68 | 33/1 | 16 | 6 | 3 | 1 | 1 | 0 | 0 | 40/1 | 20 |
| 1968/69 | 42 | 22 | 5 | 4 | 4 | 3 | 0 | 0 | 51 | 29 |
| 1969/70 | 42 | 23 | 1 | 0 | 4 | 0 | 0 | 0 | 47 | 23 |
| 1970/71 | 40 | 17 | 5 | 2 | 1 | 0 | 6 | 4 | 52 | 23 |
| 1971/72 | 26/2 | 9 | 3 | 0 | 1 | 0 | 0 | 0 | 30/2 | 9 |
| 1972/73 | 14 | 7 | 0 | 0 | 1 | 0 | 0 | 0 | 15 | 7 |
| 1973/74 | 18 | 2 | 3 | 0 | 1 | 0 | 0 | 0 | 22 | 2 |
| 1974/75 | 8 | 3 | 0 | 0 | 2 | 0 | 0 | 0 | 10 | 3 |
| | 229/3 | 102 | 23 | 9 | 15 | 4 | 6 | 4 | 273/3 | 119 |

**Honours at Everton**
Division 1 winner: 1969/70
FA Cup runner-up: 1968
Caps for England: 2
Caps for England Under-23: 10
Appearances for the Football League: 1

**Management record at Everton 1994/95-1996/97**
League: 36 wins, 31 draws, 30 defeats
FA Cup winners: 1995

# TED SAGAR

*Ted Sagar served Everton for 24 years,*
*the longest term by any player with one club.*

Nicknamed 'The Boss' by his colleagues, Sagar enjoyed an illustrious career of 24 years at Goodison Park. He was one of the most popular net-minders of all time and was the stuff of legends. Sagar had toiled in the pits from the early age of 13 and joined Everton from Thorne Colliery of the Doncaster Senior League. The goalkeeper repaid his £10 signing-on fee by establishing a club record of 499 first-team outings for the Toffees, 452 of them in Division 1. Although he did not represent a physically imposing figure, Sagar combined athleticism and lightning-quick reflexes with exemplary handling skills to command his penalty area. He patrolled his territory like a spider in a web and demonstrated incredible bravery in the days when it was legitimate for forwards to bundle both the ball and the goalkeeper into the net. Sagar kept 118 clean-sheets.

Having relinquished his regular first-team place to Jimmy O'Neill, Sagar played his final game at Plymouth Argyle in November 1952 - at the age of 42 years and 282 days. The Everton veteran collected his share of honours during his remarkable reign between 1930-1952, including two League championship medals and an FA Cup winners' medal. Sagar was also awarded four England caps, his first against Northern Ireland in 1935.

Born: Moorends, Yorkshire, 1910
Height: 1.78 m (5 ft 10 in)  Weight: 68.1 kg (10 st 10 lb)

|  | League | | FA Cup | | Other | | Total | |
|---|---|---|---|---|---|---|---|---|
|  | apps | goals | apps | goals | apps | goals | apps | goals |
| 1929/30 | 8 | 0 | 1 | 0 | 0 | 0 | 9 | 0 |
| 1931/32 | 41 | 0 | 1 | 0 | 0 | 0 | 42 | 0 |
| 1932/33 | 42 | 0 | 6 | 0 | 0 | 0 | 48 | 0 |
| 1933/34 | 40 | 0 | 1 | 0 | 0 | 0 | 41 | 0 |
| 1934/35 | 35 | 0 | 4 | 0 | 0 | 0 | 39 | 0 |
| 1935/36 | 37 | 0 | 0 | 0 | 0 | 0 | 37 | 0 |
| 1936/37 | 29 | 0 | 4 | 0 | 0 | 0 | 33 | 0 |
| 1937/38 | 26 | 0 | 0 | 0 | 3 | 0 | 29 | 0 |
| 1938/39 | 41 | 0 | 5 | 0 | 1 | 0 | 47 | 0 |
| 1946/47 | 29 | 0 | 2 | 0 | 0 | 0 | 31 | 0 |
| 1947/48 | 42 | 0 | 5 | 0 | 0 | 0 | 47 | 0 |
| 1948/49 | 40 | 0 | 2 | 0 | 0 | 0 | 42 | 0 |
| 1949/50 | 18 | 0 | 0 | 0 | 0 | 0 | 18 | 0 |
| 1950/51 | 24 | 0 | 1 | 0 | 0 | 0 | 25 | 0 |
| 1951/52 | 10 | 0 | 0 | 0 | 0 | 0 | 10 | 0 |
| 1952/53 | 1 | 0 | 0 | 0 | 0 | 0 | 1 | 0 |
| | 463 | 0 | 32 | 0 | 4 | 0 | 499 | 0 |

**Honours at Everton**
Division 1 winner: 1931/32, 1938/39
FA Cup winner: 1933
Caps for England: 4
Appearances for the Football League: 5

# BILLY SCOTT

*Billy Scott was a reliable custodian,
the safest pair of hands in his era.*

Scott was already an accomplished Ireland international when he joined Everton from Linfield for £500 in 1904. During his first season he contested the position between the posts with the more eccentric Dr Leigh Roose. Although their duel did not assist the club's attempt at a League and Cup double, Scott persevered to secure the No 1 jersey and made 289 first-team appearances for Everton between 1904/05-1911/12.

The goalkeeper was equal to the challenges of his most intimidating adversaries and dominated his penalty area. He made up for his lack of size with an abundance of courage, composure and cat-like agility. Scott established an influential relationship with centre-half Jack Taylor and was an authoritative member of the Everton teams which went very close to filling the Goodison trophy cabinet with silverware in the Edwardian era. The Toffees lifted the English Cup in 1906 but also endured a series of frustrating near-misses. Despite Scott's heroic efforts, Everton contrived to finish runners-up in Division 1 in 1904/05, 1908/09 and 1911/12 and the English Cup in 1907. They were also defeated at the semi-final stage on two other occasions.

Scott had more success at international level and was enlisted 25 times by Northern Ireland, gaining 16 of these caps during his Goodison career. He was a role model for his younger brother Elisha Scott, who joined Liverpool in 1912 and subsequently provided sterling service to the Reds for over two decades. That same year, the Everton goalkeeper defected to Leeds City while still at the peak of his game. He gained three more caps with the ill-fated Yorkshire-club. Scott later played 27 times for Liverpool in regional football during the 1918/19 season.

Born: Belfast, 1884
Height: 1.78 m (5 ft 10 in) Weight: 69.9 kg (11 st 0 lb)

| | League | | FA Cup | | Total | |
|---|---|---|---|---|---|---|
| | apps | goals | apps | goals | apps | goals |
| 1904/05 | 16 | 0 | 0 | 0 | 16 | 0 |
| 1905/06 | 35 | 0 | 6 | 0 | 41 | 0 |
| 1906/07 | 35 | 0 | 8 | 0 | 43 | 0 |
| 1907/08 | 34 | 0 | 7 | 0 | 41 | 0 |
| 1908/09 | 36 | 0 | 2 | 0 | 38 | 0 |
| 1909/10 | 27 | 0 | 7 | 0 | 34 | 0 |
| 1910/11 | 31 | 0 | 3 | 0 | 34 | 0 |
| 1911/12 | 37 | 0 | 5 | 0 | 42 | 0 |
| | 251 | 0 | 38 | 0 | 289 | 0 |

**Honours at Everton**
Division 1 runner-up: 1904/05, 1908/09, 1911/12
FA Cup (English Cup ) winner: 1906
FA Cup (English Cup) runner-up: 1907
Caps for Ireland: 16

# JIMMY SETTLE

*Jimmy Settle was one of the instinctive
goal-poachers of Edwardian football.*

Settle had turned out for Bolton Wanderers, Halliwell Rovers and Bury before succumbing to the attraction of Everton in 1899. The 23-year old inside-left had already tasted international stardom with Bury and, as a result, cost Everton a fee of £400. He was an instant success on Merseyside and became one of the first household names of professional football.

Standing 1.67 m, Settle was small but tough and developed into a master of glittering footwork and defence-splitting passes. But perhaps the diminutive inside-forward was most revered for his explosive acceleration, which was reputed to have left opponents rooted to the spot. He was also an instinctive finisher and averaged more than one goal in every three games.

A native of Cumberland, Settle enjoyed an illustrious career on Merseyside and was an important member of the first Everton team to win the English Cup. Although he was unfortunate not to capture more prizes during his time at Goodison, the England star was selected for international duty on three occasions shortly after the turn of the century. He played at outside-left on all of his international outings, amazingly he had occupied that position only once for Everton. Settle moved to Stockport County in 1908.

Born: Millom, Cumberland, 1875
Height: 1.67 m (5 ft 6 in) Weight: 69.5 kg (10 st 13 lb)

| | League apps | goals | FA Cup apps | goals | Total apps | goals |
|---|---|---|---|---|---|---|
| 1898/99 | 1 | 0 | 0 | 0 | 1 | 0 |
| 1899/00 | 26 | 10 | 1 | 0 | 27 | 10 |
| 1900/01 | 30 | 10 | 2 | 1 | 32 | 11 |
| 1901/02 | 29 | 18 | 0 | 0 | 29 | 18 |
| 1902/03 | 20 | 5 | 2 | 0 | 22 | 5 |
| 1903/04 | 29 | 8 | 1 | 0 | 30 | 8 |
| 1904/05 | 32 | 9 | 6 | 4 | 38 | 13 |
| 1905/06 | 28 | 11 | 5 | 1 | 33 | 12 |
| 1906/07 | 21 | 6 | 8 | 4 | 29 | 10 |
| 1907/08 | 21 | 7 | 7 | 3 | 28 | 10 |
| | 237 | 84 | 32 | 13 | 269 | 97 |

**Honours at Everton**
FA Cup (English Cup) winner: 1906
FA Cup (English Cup) runner-up: 1907
Division 1 runner-up: 1901/02, 1904/05
Caps for England: 3
Appearances for the Football League: 2

# GRAEME SHARP

*Sharp was an outstanding striker,*
*acclaimed for his spectacular goals.*

Sharp was considered to be a long-term investment when Gordon Lee signed him from Dumbarton for £120,000. The raw teenager broke into the first-team squad within 18 months and impressed the Goodison fans with his exciting play. Ideally built for the challenges faced by a modern front-man and expert at shielding the ball in the tightest situations, Sharp was dangerous in the air and packed an explosive shot.

He fine-tuned his game to accommodate the strengths of his partners and enjoyed productive pairings with Adrian Heath, Andy Gray, Gary Lineker and Tony Cottee. Sharp scored 158 goals during his 11 glorious seasons and occupies second place on Everton's list of all-time marksmen. Although none of his strikes was more rewarding than the first goal in the 1984 FA Cup final, possibly his best effort was reserved for Anfield in 1984 when he lashed the ball home from way outside of the penalty area.

The elegant striker was awarded 12 caps by Scotland but failed to fully reproduce his club form at international level. He was transferred to Oldham Athletic for £500,000 in 1991 and subsequently managed the Boundary Park-club as well as Bangor City.

Born: Glasgow, 1960
Height: 1.85 m (6 ft 1 in)  Weight: 73.5 kg (11 st 8 lb)

|         | League apps | goals | FA Cup apps | goals | Other apps | goals | Europe apps | goals | Total apps | goals |
|---------|------|-----|------|-----|------|-----|------|-----|--------|-----|
| 1979/80 | 1/1  | 0   | 0    | 0   | 0    | 0   | 0    | 0   | 1/1    | 0   |
| 1980/81 | 2/2  | 0   | 0    | 0   | 0    | 0   | 0    | 0   | 2/2    | 0   |
| 1981/82 | 27/2 | 15  | 1    | 0   | 1    | 0   | 0    | 0   | 29/2   | 15  |
| 1982/83 | 39/2 | 15  | 5    | 2   | 4    | 0   | 0    | 0   | 48/2   | 17  |
| 1983/84 | 27/1 | 7   | 5/2  | 1   | 11   | 3   | 0    | 0   | 43/3   | 11  |
| 1984/85 | 36   | 21  | 6    | 2   | 5    | 3   | 8    | 4   | 55     | 30  |
| 1985/86 | 35/2 | 19  | 7    | 1   | 11/1 | 3   | 0    | 0   | 53/3   | 23  |
| 1986/87 | 27   | 5   | 1    | 2   | 7    | 5   | 0    | 0   | 35     | 12  |
| 1987/88 | 32   | 13  | 8    | 6   | 8/1  | 3   | 0    | 0   | 48/1   | 22  |
| 1988/89 | 26   | 7   | 6    | 3   | 6    | 3   | 0    | 0   | 38     | 13  |
| 1989/90 | 30/3 | 6   | 7    | 1   | 4/1  | 0   | 0    | 0   | 41/4   | 7   |
| 1990/91 | 24/3 | 3   | 6    | 2   | 3    | 3   | 0    | 0   | 33/3   | 8   |
|         | 306/16 | 111 | 52/2 | 20 | 60/3 | 23 | 8 | 4 | 426/21 | 158 |

**Honours at Everton**
Division 1 winner: 1984/85, 1986/87
Division 1 runner-up: 1985/86
European Cup-Winners' Cup winner: 1985
FA Cup winner: 1984
FA Cup runner-up: 1985, 1986, 1989
Milk Cup runner-up: 1983/84
Simod Cup runner-up: 1988/89
Screen Sport Super Cup runner-up: 1985/86
Caps for Scotland: 12
Caps for Scotland Under-21: 1

# JACK SHARP

*Jack Sharp represented England at both football and cricket.*

Sharp played for Hereford Thistle and Aston Villa before moving on to Everton as a 20-year old in 1899. The powerfully-built outside-right was a genuine speed merchant, famed for his brilliant ball control. He was also a respected goal-scorer finding the target on 80 occasions during his Goodison career. Sharp demonstrated courage, intelligence and class in everything that he did and played in English Cup finals with Everton in 1906 and 1907. Predictably, he impressed the England selectors and was awarded two international caps, the first against Ireland in 1903. He also represented the Football League on three occasions before retiring in 1910.

Like his Everton team-mate Harry Makepeace, Sharp was an England international at both football and cricket. In fact, the distinguished cricketer had relocated to Merseyside to obtain residential qualifications to play for Lancashire County CC. He became a mainstay in the Lancashire team between 1899-1925. He amassed 22,715 runs including 38 centuries, took 448 wickets and held 236 catches during his first-class cricket career of 534 matches and 805 innings. Sharp was awarded three England caps and scored 105 against Australia at the Oval in 1909.

This football and cricket international ran a sports outfitting business in Whitechapel, Liverpool for many years and became an Everton director in 1922.

Born: Hereford, 1878
Height: 1.68 m (5 ft 6 in)  Weight: 73.5 kg (11 st 8 lb)

|  | League apps | League goals | FA Cup apps | FA Cup goals | Total apps | Total goals |
|---|---|---|---|---|---|---|
| 1899/00 | 29 | 5 | 1 | 0 | 30 | 5 |
| 1900/01 | 25 | 7 | 2 | 0 | 27 | 7 |
| 1901/02 | 32 | 6 | 2 | 1 | 34 | 7 |
| 1902/03 | 27 | 6 | 2 | 1 | 29 | 7 |
| 1903/04 | 31 | 6 | 1 | 0 | 32 | 6 |
| 1904/05 | 21 | 8 | 6 | 2 | 27 | 10 |
| 1905/06 | 29 | 9 | 6 | 2 | 35 | 11 |
| 1906/07 | 27 | 7 | 6 | 3 | 33 | 10 |
| 1907/08 | 23 | 4 | 7 | 0 | 30 | 4 |
| 1908/09 | 31 | 6 | 2 | 1 | 33 | 7 |
| 1909/10 | 25 | 4 | 7 | 2 | 32 | 6 |
|  | 300 | 68 | 42 | 12 | 342 | 80 |

**Honours at Everton**
FA Cup (English Cup) winner: 1906
FA Cup (English Cup) runner-up: 1907
Division 1 runner-up: 1901/02, 1904/05, 1908/09
Caps for England: 2
Appearances for the Football League: 3

# KEVIN SHEEDY

*Kevin Sheedy was a dead-ball specialist
with a magic wand of a left-foot.*

After kicking off his career with Hereford United, Sheedy was languishing in Liverpool's Central League team when he caught the eye of Everton manager Howard Kendall. Although the talented mid-fielder had made only two senior appearances in four seasons, Liverpool were reluctant to lose him to their neighbours and the transfer fee had to be set by a tribunal. The £100,000 transaction proved to be money well spent.

Sheedy created many goals with his laser-accurate passing and conjured up dozens of his own via his fearsome long-distance shooting. The Goodison favourite developed into a dead-ball specialist and dispatched free-kicks with surgical precision. He scored one of his most important goals in the 1985 European Cup-Winners' Cup final.

Sheedy wrestled for fitness throughout his decade at Goodison. Niggling injuries limited him to only 60% of possible League games and prevented him from participating in the 1984 FA Cup final triumph. In total, he had nine outings at Wembley with Everton, but was substituted on four occasions. But despite his frailty, Sheedy was a consistent performer and his subtle skills made significant contributions to Everton's dominance in the mid-1980s. He was rewarded with 41 caps by the Republic of Ireland before moving to Newcastle United on a free transfer in 1992. Sheedy signed for Blackpool 12 months later and subsequently started his coaching career with Tranmere Rovers.

Born: Builth Wells, 1959
Height: 1.78 m (5 ft 10 in)  Weight: 69.5 kg (10 st 13 lb)

| | League apps | League goals | FA Cup apps | FA Cup goals | Other apps | Other goals | Europe apps | Europe goals | Total apps | Total goals |
|---|---|---|---|---|---|---|---|---|---|---|
| 1982/83 | 40 | 11 | 5 | 2 | 3 | 0 | 0 | 0 | 48 | 13 |
| 1983/84 | 28 | 4 | 6 | 2 | 10 | 4 | 0 | 0 | 44 | 10 |
| 1984/85 | 29 | 11 | 6 | 4 | 2 | 0 | 5 | 2 | 42 | 17 |
| 1985/86 | 31 | 5 | 3 | 0 | 11 | 5 | 0 | 0 | 45 | 10 |
| 1986/87 | 28 | 13 | 1 | 0 | 6 | 2 | 0 | 0 | 35 | 15 |
| 1987/88 | 14/3 | 1 | 0 | 0 | 4 | 0 | 0 | 0 | 18/3 | 1 |
| 1988/89 | 24/2 | 8 | 8 | 4 | 6/1 | 0 | 0 | 0 | 38/3 | 12 |
| 1989/90 | 33/4 | 9 | 6 | 2 | 4 | 2 | 0 | 0 | 43/4 | 13 |
| 1990/91 | 20/2 | 4 | 3 | 1 | 3 | 0 | 0 | 0 | 26/2 | 5 |
| 1991/92 | 16/1 | 0 | 0 | 0 | 3 | 0 | 0 | 0 | 19/1 | 0 |
| | 263/12 | 66 | 38 | 15 | 52/1 | 13 | 5 | 2 | 358/13 | 96 |

**Honours at Everton**
Division 1 winner:  1984/85, 1986/87
Division 1 runner-up:  1985/86
European Cup-Winners' Cup winner:  1985
FA Cup runner-up:  1985, 1986, 1989
Milk Cup runner-up:  1983/84
Simod Cup runner-up:  1988/89
Zenith Data Systems Cup runner-up:  1990/91
Screen Sport Super Cup runner-up:  1985/86
Caps for Eire:  41

# NEVILLE SOUTHALL

*Neville Southall played more games for club and country than any other Evertonian.*

Southall had spells with Llandudno Swifts, Conwy United, Bangor City, Winsford United and Bury before joining Everton for £150,000. After a nine-game loan spell at Port Vale, he contested the goalkeeping job with Jim Arnold before becoming the unopposed Everton No 1 in 1983 and for the next 14 seasons.

The Wales star's superb anticipation and spectacular reflexes made him the finest goalkeeper in the world in the mid-1980s. His rumpled exterior camouflaged his perfectionism as he kept 272 clean-sheets for Everton. Southall earned a record of 92 caps for Wales as well as world-wide fame. He was voted FWA 'Footballer of the Year' in 1985 and honoured with the MBE in 1996. After leaving Goodison, he played for Southend United, Stoke City, Doncaster Rovers and Torquay United.

Born: Llandudno, 1958
Height: 1.85 m (6 ft 1 in)  Weight: 93.0 kg (14 st 7 lb)

| | League apps | goals | FA Cup apps | goals | Other apps | goals | Europe apps | goals | Total apps | goals |
|---|---|---|---|---|---|---|---|---|---|---|
| 1981/82 | 26 | 0 | 1 | 0 | 0 | 0 | 0 | 0 | 27 | 0 |
| 1982/83 | 17 | 0 | 0 | 0 | 2 | 0 | 0 | 0 | 19 | 0 |
| 1983/84 | 35 | 0 | 8 | 0 | 11 | 0 | 0 | 0 | 54 | 0 |
| 1984/85 | 42 | 0 | 7 | 0 | 5 | 0 | 9 | 0 | 63 | 0 |
| 1985/86 | 32 | 0 | 5 | 0 | 12 | 0 | 0 | 0 | 49 | 0 |
| 1986/87 | 31 | 0 | 3 | 0 | 5 | 0 | 0 | 0 | 39 | 0 |
| 1987/88 | 32 | 0 | 8 | 0 | 9 | 0 | 0 | 0 | 49 | 0 |
| 1988/89 | 38 | 0 | 8 | 0 | 9 | 0 | 0 | 0 | 55 | 0 |
| 1989/90 | 38 | 0 | 7 | 0 | 4 | 0 | 0 | 0 | 49 | 0 |
| 1990/91 | 38 | 0 | 6 | 0 | 9 | 0 | 0 | 0 | 53 | 0 |
| 1991/92 | 42 | 0 | 2 | 0 | 6 | 0 | 0 | 0 | 50 | 0 |
| 1992/93 | 40 | 0 | 1 | 0 | 6 | 0 | 0 | 0 | 47 | 0 |
| 1993/94 | 42 | 0 | 2 | 0 | 4 | 0 | 0 | 0 | 48 | 0 |
| 1994/95 | 41 | 0 | 6 | 0 | 2 | 0 | 0 | 0 | 49 | 0 |
| 1995/96 | 38 | 0 | 4 | 0 | 3 | 0 | 4 | 0 | 49 | 0 |
| 1996/97 | 34 | 0 | 2 | 0 | 2 | 0 | 0 | 0 | 38 | 0 |
| 1997/98 | 12 | 0 | 0 | 0 | 1 | 0 | 0 | 0 | 13 | 0 |
| | 578 | 0 | 70 | 0 | 90 | 0 | 13 | 0 | 751 | 0 |

**Honours at Everton**
Division 1 winner: 1984/85, 1986/87
Division 1 runner-up: 1985/86
European Cup-Winners' Cup winner: 1985
FA Cup winner: 1984, 1995
FA Cup runner-up: 1985, 1989
Milk Cup runner-up: 1983/84
Simod Cup runner-up: 1988/89
Zenith Data Systems Cup runner-up: 1990/91
Caps for Wales: 92
Appearances for the Football League: 1

# JACK SOUTHWORTH

*Jack Southworth had the uncanny knack
of turning half-chances into goals.*

Having unexpectedly lost the 1893 English Cup final to Wolverhampton Wanderers, Everton sought a star attraction to revive their fortunes. Accordingly they acquired Southworth, the biggest name in the evolving professional era. The England international centre-forward had established a nation-wide reputation as a prolific goal-scorer with Blackburn Olympic and Blackburn Rovers and had earned English Cup winners' medals with Blackburn Rovers in 1890 and 1891.

Although Everton were required to pay a handsome fee of £400 for his signature, they received good value from their investment. Southworth thrilled the packed crowds at the newly-constructed Goodison Park with his dazzling dribbling skills and registered 36 goals during his brief stay of 31 League games with Everton. Without question, he hit his peak over the 1893 Christmas period when the star centre-forward drove the Goodison congregation delirious with 10 goals in seven days, including four in the 8-1 thrashing of Sheffield Wednesday and six more in the 7-1 defeat of West Bromwich Albion. But inexplicably his expert marksmanship failed to deliver any major silverware.

The Toffees kicked off the 1894/95 season with Southworth in tremendous form. They dominated the title race until he was seriously injured against Sunderland, the eventual League champions. Sadly Southworth never played professional football again. Throughout his truncated career he had demonstrated the abilities and instincts of a forward of rare quality, averaging 1.125 goals per game with Everton. Southworth had been awarded three England caps, rattling in three goals for his country, and had also represented the Football League before moving to Merseyside. But he earned no further international honours at Everton.

After injury had forced Southworth into premature retirement, he became a professional violinist with the Hallé Orchestra and the Royal Liverpool Philharmonic Orchestra.

Born: Blackburn, 1866
Height: 1.73 m (5 ft 8 in)  Weight: 71.3 kg (11 st 3 lb)

|  | League apps | League goals | FA Cup apps | FA Cup goals | Total apps | Total goals |
|---|---|---|---|---|---|---|
| 1893/94 | 22 | 27 | 1 | 0 | 23 | 27 |
| 1894/95 | 9 | 9 | 0 | 0 | 9 | 9 |
|  | 31 | 36 | 1 | 0 | 32 | 36 |

# JIMMY STEIN

*Jimmy Stein was a model professional
highly respected by his peers.*

Stein followed the well-worn trail over Hadrian's Wall to Goodison Park in 1928.
The outside-left had helped Dunfermline win the Scottish League Division 2 title and
was recruited by Everton to replace Scotland international Alec Troup. Something of
a bargain buy at £1,400, Stein enjoyed a rewarding career of more than six seasons
on Merseyside and became a key member of the all-conquering Everton teams which
won the Division 2 crown in 1930/31, Division 1 championship in 1931/32 and
FA Cup in 1933, for the first-time in 27 years.

Tall for a winger, Stein was celebrated for his sheer pace and his ability to ride tackles.
He liked to link up with inside-left Tosh Johnson and provide service to centre-forward
Dixie Dean or alternatively cut inside to deliver telling strikes. His powerful shooting
resulted in a rich harvest of 65 goals during his time at Goodison. In fact, Stein scored
five times in the 1933 FA Cup campaign and emerged as one of the important figures
in the conquest of Manchester City in the final by grabbing the opening goal in
the Wembley triumph.

Stein was respected by his team-mates and the Goodison fans as a model professional
devoted to the royal blue cause. Towards the end of his career, Stein was forced to
contest his first-team spot with big-money signings such as Jackie Coulter from Belfast
Celtic and Torry Gillick from Glasgow Rangers. As a result, his Division 1 outings
became less frequent but he never complained. Subsequently, Stein was transferred
to Burnley in 1936 and later played for New Brighton of Division 3 (North).

Born: Coatbridge, 1907
Height: 1.78 m (5 ft 10 in)  Weight: 74.5 kg (11 st 10 lb)

|  | League apps | goals | FA Cup apps | goals | Other apps | goals | Total apps | goals |
|---|---|---|---|---|---|---|---|---|
| 1928/29 | 4 | 0 | 1 | 0 | 0 | 0 | 5 | 0 |
| 1929/30 | 29 | 10 | 2 | 0 | 0 | 0 | 31 | 10 |
| 1930/31 | 28 | 10 | 5 | 3 | 0 | 0 | 33 | 13 |
| 1931/32 | 37 | 9 | 1 | 0 | 0 | 0 | 38 | 9 |
| 1932/33 | 40 | 16 | 6 | 5 | 1 | 0 | 47 | 21 |
| 1933/34 | 42 | 8 | 1 | 0 | 1 | 0 | 44 | 8 |
| 1934/35 | 19 | 4 | 0 | 0 | 0 | 0 | 19 | 4 |
|  | 199 | 57 | 16 | 8 | 2 | 0 | 217 | 65 |

**Honours at Everton**
Division 1 winner: 1931/32
Division 2 winner: 1930/31
FA Cup winner: 1933

# TREVOR STEVEN

*Trevor Steven was a gifted ball-player who won titles in England, Scotland and France.*

Everton manager Howard Kendall coveted Steven for two years before securing his transfer from Burnley in 1983. The 20-year old did not come cheap at £300,000 but developed into one of the finest footballers that Everton have ever had on their books. Steven not only influenced games with his sublime football skills and intelligence, but was also prepared to couple these qualities with honest endeavour and toiled in mid-field, denying spaces to the opposition and covering for Gary Stevens when the full-back ventured forward. In addition to his scintillating ball skills, Steven was renowned for his abilities to shimmy past opponents and lacerate defences with calibrated passes. He possessed the rare talent of producing the killer pass. Although regarded more of a provider than a finisher, the stylish footballer netted important goals against Bayern Munich in the semi-final and against Rapid Vienna in the final of the European Cup-Winners' Cup. In fact, Steven finished top-scorer with 14 League goals when Everton regained the Division 1 title in 1986/87.

Acknowledged as the most skillful member of Everton's most successful team of all time, Steven gained his first England call-up in 1984 against Northern Ireland. He chalked up 25 international caps during his Goodison career before enjoying further success in Scotland and France. The 26-year old star was sold to Glasgow Rangers in 1989, the modest fee of £1.525 million being established at a tribunal. Two years later he moved to Marseille (France) for £4.5 million. Steven subsequently rejoined the Ibrox Park-club and enjoyed further success. He won the Scottish title in each of his seven seasons with Glasgow Rangers.

Born: Berwick upon Tweed, 1963
Height: 1.73 m (5 ft 8 in) Weight: 70.8 kg (11 st 2 lb)

|  | League apps | goals | FA Cup apps | goals | Other apps | goals | Europe apps | goals | Total apps | goals |
|---|---|---|---|---|---|---|---|---|---|---|
| 1983/84 | 23/4 | 1 | 2 | 0 | 3 | 1 | 0 | 0 | 28/4 | 2 |
| 1984/85 | 40 | 12 | 7 | 2 | 5 | 0 | 9 | 2 | 61 | 16 |
| 1985/86 | 41 | 9 | 6 | 0 | 13 | 1 | 0 | 0 | 60 | 10 |
| 1986/87 | 41 | 14 | 3 | 0 | 8 | 2 | 0 | 0 | 52 | 16 |
| 1987/88 | 36 | 6 | 8 | 2 | 7 | 0 | 0 | 0 | 51 | 8 |
| 1988/89 | 29 | 6 | 7 | 0 | 7 | 2 | 0 | 0 | 43 | 8 |
|  | 210/4 | 48 | 33 | 4 | 43 | 6 | 9 | 2 | 295/4 | 60 |

**Honours at Everton**
Division 1 winner: 1984/85, 1986/87
Division 1 runner-up: 1985/86
European Cup-Winners' Cup winner: 1985
FA Cup winner: 1984
FA Cup runner-up: 1985, 1986, 1989
Simod Cup runner-up: 1988/89
Screen Sport Super Cup runner-up: 1985/86
Caps for England: 25
Caps for England Under-21: 2

# GARY STEVENS

*Gary Stevens was one of the fastest defenders of his generation.*

Stevens rose through the ranks of the Goodison youth development programme to make his senior debut as an 18-year old. He claimed the right-back berth in preference to Brian Burrows in 1982 and went on to make nearly 300 appearances for the club in the 1980s. The reliable defender played an important part in Everton's rise from their turn-of-the-decade doldrums to nearly clinching an unprecedented treble in 1985 and featured in two league championship campaigns, four Wembley finals and a European triumph.

Stevens epitomised the modern full-back - a superb athlete equipped with blazing pace and crisp tackles. He liked to make overlapping forays up his beat in support of his forwards and was at his best when raiding deep into enemy territory. The Everton defender also frustrated opponents with his deceptive speed of recovery and was rarely stranded up-field. His only possible shortcoming was his occasionally wayward ball distribution.

The England full-back represented his country in the 1986 World Cup tournament in Mexico and in total gained 26 international caps, his first appearance was against Italy in 1985. Although he was still in his prime, Stevens was sold to Glasgow Rangers for £1.25 million in 1988. Six years later he returned to Merseyside ladened with Scottish silver and provided stalwart service to Tranmere Rovers.

Born: Barrow in Furness, 1963
Height: 1.80 m (5 ft 11 in) Weight: 73.0 kg (11 st 7 lb)

| | League apps | goals | FA Cup apps | goals | Other apps | goals | Europe apps | goals | Total apps | goals |
|---|---|---|---|---|---|---|---|---|---|---|
| 1981/82 | 19 | 1 | 1 | 0 | 4 | 0 | 0 | 0 | 24 | 1 |
| 1982/83 | 28 | 0 | 5 | 0 | 2 | 1 | 0 | 0 | 35 | 1 |
| 1983/84 | 26/1 | 1 | 8 | 0 | 8 | 0 | 0 | 0 | 42/1 | 1 |
| 1984/85 | 37 | 3 | 7 | 1 | 5 | 0 | 9 | 0 | 58 | 4 |
| 1985/86 | 41 | 1 | 6 | 1 | 11 | 0 | 0 | 0 | 58 | 2 |
| 1986/87 | 25 | 2 | 3 | 0 | 1 | 0 | 0 | 0 | 29 | 2 |
| 1987/88 | 31 | 0 | 8 | 0 | 7 | 1 | 0 | 0 | 46 | 1 |
| | 207/1 | 8 | 38 | 2 | 38 | 2 | 9 | 0 | 292/1 | 12 |

**Honours at Everton**
Division 1 winner: 1984/85, 1986/87
Division 1 runner-up: 1985/86
European Cup-Winners' Cup: 1985
FA Cup winner: 1984
FA Cup runner-up: 1985, 1986
Milk Cup runner-up: 1983/84
Caps for England: 26
Caps for England 'B': 1
Caps for England Under-21: 1

# ALEX STEVENSON

*Alex Stevenson illuminated Goodison Park*
*with his dazzling footwork.*

The Irish star had tasted success in the Scottish League with Glasgow Rangers before moving to Merseyside. Nevertheless, the 22-year old pledged his future to Everton in 1934 and proved to be an inspired acquisition at £2,750.

Stevenson packed an abundance of rich talents into his compact frame. Although only 1.60 m tall, he was tough enough to withstand the fiercest tackles and harassment. The little inside-forward displayed immaculate technique and was hailed as one of the finest ball-players of his generation. Stevenson was the brains behind Everton's domination of Division 1 immediately before World War II. His sparkling partnership with fellow Irishman Jackie Coulter tore defences to shreds. Their speedy interplay and telepathic understanding with centre-forward Tommy Lawton overwhelmed opponents and were rewarded with a League championship success in 1938/39.

Stevenson's career spanned 16 seasons but was severely disrupted by World War II. He made 275 appearances for the Toffees between 1933/34-1948/49 plus another 205 outings in war-time competitions. Stevenson collected his quota of international honours, earning 6 caps with Eire and 14 caps for Northern Ireland during his time at Goodison. Previously, he had represented Eire during his early days with Dublin Dolphins, his first professional club. Stevenson enjoyed a lengthy international career. His final cap was awarded some 18 years after receiving his first call-up. Stevenson retired in 1949 and became player-manager at Bootle two years later.

Born: Dublin, 1912
Height: 1.60 m (5 ft 3 in)  Weight: 66.3 kg (10 st 6 lb)

| | League apps | League goals | FA Cup apps | FA Cup goals | Other apps | Other goals | Total apps | Total goals |
|---|---|---|---|---|---|---|---|---|
| 1933/34 | 12 | 1 | 0 | 0 | 0 | 0 | 12 | 1 |
| 1934/35 | 36 | 15 | 5 | 3 | 0 | 0 | 41 | 18 |
| 1935/36 | 29 | 10 | 0 | 0 | 0 | 0 | 29 | 10 |
| 1936/37 | 41 | 19 | 3 | 2 | 0 | 0 | 44 | 21 |
| 1937/38 | 35 | 13 | 2 | 1 | 3 | 0 | 40 | 14 |
| 1938/39 | 36 | 11 | 5 | 2 | 1 | 1 | 42 | 14 |
| 1946/47 | 30 | 8 | 0 | 0 | 0 | 0 | 30 | 8 |
| 1947/48 | 17 | 3 | 0 | 0 | 0 | 0 | 17 | 3 |
| 1948/49 | 19 | 2 | 1 | 0 | 0 | 0 | 20 | 2 |
| | 255 | 82 | 16 | 8 | 4 | 1 | 275 | 91 |

**Honours at Everton**
Division 1 winner: 1938/39
Caps for Northern Ireland: 14
Caps for Eire: 6
War-time appearances for Northern Ireland: 1

# JACK TAYLOR

*Jack Taylor was the favourite Evertonian of his era and first captain to lift the FA Cup.*

After stints with Newtown Thistle, Dumbarton Athletic and Paisley St Mirren, Taylor journeyed south to Everton in 1896. He developed into one of the finest centre-halves in the country and one of Everton's all-time greats.

Taylor threw his heart and soul as well as every ounce of his energy into every game. These qualities made him one of the most popular Evertonians of all time and the most versatile player of his era. In fact, Taylor was the forerunner of the modern utility player and occupied seven positions during his 14 seasons at the club. He featured at outside-right in the 1897 English Cup final and returned to the Crystal Palace venue in 1906 at centre-half and club captain. Taylor lifted the English Cup for the first-time in Everton's history after the 1-0 victory over Newcastle United. Upon returning to Merseyside, he found great pride in displaying the trophy from the driver's seat of a four-in-hand carriage.

Prior to moving to Merseyside, Taylor had collected four Scotland caps and had also represented the Scottish League on six occasions. But remarkably, he received no further honours during his Goodison days. Taylor was denied a longer playing career by a freak accident in the 1910 semi-final replay when he sustained serious damage to his larynx. Reluctantly, he moved to South Liverpool later that season. Taylor died after a motoring accident in 1949.

Born: Dumbarton, 1872
Height: 1.78 m (5 ft 10 in)  Weight: 73.1 kg (11 st 7 lb)

|  | League apps | League goals | FA Cup apps | FA Cup goals | Total apps | Total goals |
|---|---|---|---|---|---|---|
| 1896/97 | 30 | 13 | 5 | 2 | 35 | 15 |
| 1897/98 | 30 | 3 | 5 | 3 | 35 | 6 |
| 1898/99 | 34 | 3 | 2 | 1 | 36 | 4 |
| 1899/00 | 32 | 7 | 1 | 0 | 33 | 7 |
| 1900/01 | 25 | 11 | 2 | 1 | 27 | 12 |
| 1901/02 | 26 | 8 | 2 | 0 | 28 | 8 |
| 1902/03 | 33 | 3 | 3 | 1 | 36 | 4 |
| 1903/04 | 22 | 6 | 1 | 1 | 23 | 7 |
| 1904/05 | 34 | 4 | 6 | 0 | 40 | 4 |
| 1905/06 | 36 | 4 | 6 | 2 | 42 | 6 |
| 1906/07 | 34 | 1 | 8 | 2 | 42 | 3 |
| 1907/08 | 23 | 2 | 7 | 0 | 30 | 2 |
| 1908/09 | 27 | 1 | 1 | 0 | 28 | 1 |
| 1909/10 | 14 | 0 | 7 | 1 | 21 | 1 |
| | 400 | 66 | 56 | 14 | 456 | 80 |

**Honours at Everton**
Division 1 runner-up: 1901/02, 1904/05, 1908/09
FA Cup (English Cup) winner: 1906
FA Cup (English Cup) runner-up: 1897, 1907

# DEREK TEMPLE

*'Shirley' Temple scored probably the most celebrated goal in the club's history.*

Temple was a free-scoring local schoolboy when he signed professional forms with Everton in 1956. He continued his sensational goal-scoring exploits with the club's junior teams and made his first-team debut in 1957. However, the young forward's progress was slowed by National Service commitments in Kenya. Temple developed into a resourceful footballer and filled all the forward positions at one time or another during his Goodison career.

He was strong and mobile and also possessed explosive shooting power. Although injury limited him to only a handful of outings during the 1962/63 championship season, Temple recovered to leave an indelible mark in the club's history. The pinnacle of his career came 15 minutes from the end of the 1966 FA Cup final against Sheffield Wednesday at Wembley. Shortly after Everton had fought back from a 0-2 deficit through two important strikes from Mike Trebilcock, Temple latched on to a defensive error by Gerry Young and carried the ball unchallenged for 30 metres before firing an unstoppable shot from the edge of the penalty area past England international Ron Springett. His goal brought the trophy back to Goodison Park after an absence of 33 years and earned the left-winger an eternal place in Everton folklore.

Temple was called up by England against West Germany in 1965. After 12 seasons with Everton, he was sold to Preston North End for £35,000.

Born: Liverpool, 1938
Height: 1.73 m (5 ft 8 in)  Weight: 68.1 kg (10 st 10 lb)

| | League | | FA Cup | | Other | | Europe | | Total | |
|---|---|---|---|---|---|---|---|---|---|---|
| | apps | goals | apps | goals | apps | goals | apps | goals | apps | goals |
| 1956/57 | 7 | 3 | 0 | 0 | 0 | 0 | 0 | 0 | 7 | 3 |
| 1957/58 | 28 | 8 | 1 | 0 | 0 | 0 | 0 | 0 | 29 | 8 |
| 1958/59 | 4 | 2 | 0 | 0 | 0 | 0 | 0 | 0 | 4 | 2 |
| 1960/61 | 20 | 4 | 0 | 0 | 3 | 0 | 0 | 0 | 23 | 4 |
| 1961/62 | 17 | 10 | 0 | 0 | 0 | 0 | 0 | 0 | 17 | 10 |
| 1962/63 | 5 | 1 | 0 | 0 | 0 | 0 | 0 | 0 | 5 | 1 |
| 1963/64 | 41 | 12 | 5 | 0 | 1 | 1 | 2 | 0 | 49 | 13 |
| 1964/65 | 39 | 11 | 4 | 1 | 0 | 0 | 6 | 2 | 49 | 14 |
| 1965/66 | 38 | 9 | 8 | 6 | 0 | 0 | 4 | 0 | 50 | 15 |
| 1966/67 | 27/1 | 12 | 3 | 1 | 1 | 0 | 4 | 0 | 35/1 | 13 |
| 1967/68 | 5 | 0 | 0 | 0 | 1 | 0 | 0 | 0 | 6 | 0 |
| | 231/1 | 72 | 21 | 8 | 6 | 1 | 16 | 2 | 274/1 | 83 |

**Honours at Everton**
FA Cup winner: 1966
Caps for England: 1
Appearances for the Football League: 2

# JOCK THOMSON

*Jock Thomson's endeavours were rewarded*
*with an impressive collection of honours.*

A product of Scottish junior football with Thornton Rangers, Thomson was signed by Everton from Dundee for a fee of £3,850 in 1930. He was thrown in at the deep end with a royal blue team mired in a relegation dog-fight. But despite his efforts, the Toffees were demoted for the first time in their history. Thomson's roller-coaster ride continued for three more seasons as he experienced the joy of promotion back to the top flight in his first full season, the elation of a Division 1 championship and the ecstasy of a Wembley triumph.

A strong and forceful left-half, Thomson toiled in the Goodison mid-field trenches and strove to do the simple things well. He relished the heat of the battle and was respected for his resolute tackling which helped shore up a far from water-tight rearguard. Also his cunning passes carved out numerous goal-scoring openings for the likes of Dixie Dean and Tommy Lawton. Although he conceded his first-team place to Joe Mercer for several seasons, Thomson returned as Everton captain for the 1938/39 season and led one of the club's most accomplished sides to another League championship title. But like many of his contemporaries, his playing career was essentially terminated by the outbreak of hostilities in 1939. He guested for Carnoustie Panmuir, Aldershot and Fulham in war-time fixtures.

Thomson was capped by Scotland against Wales in 1932, but unfortunately put through his own goal and was never selected again. Immediately after World War II, he was appointed coach by Everton. He later managed Manchester City.

Born: Thornton, Fifeshire, 1906
Height: 1.83 m (6 ft 0 in) Weight: 82.4 kg (13 st 0 lb)

| | League apps | goals | FA Cup apps | goals | Other apps | goals | Total apps | goals |
|---|---|---|---|---|---|---|---|---|
| 1929/30 | 9 | 0 | 0 | 0 | 0 | 0 | 9 | 0 |
| 1930/31 | 41 | 0 | 5 | 0 | 0 | 0 | 46 | 0 |
| 1931/32 | 39 | 0 | 1 | 0 | 0 | 0 | 40 | 0 |
| 1932/33 | 41 | 3 | 6 | 0 | 1 | 0 | 48 | 3 |
| 1933/34 | 38 | 0 | 1 | 0 | 1 | 0 | 40 | 0 |
| 1934/35 | 42 | 1 | 5 | 0 | 0 | 0 | 47 | 1 |
| 1935/36 | 25 | 0 | 0 | 0 | 0 | 0 | 25 | 0 |
| 1936/37 | 2 | 0 | 0 | 0 | 0 | 0 | 2 | 0 |
| 1937/38 | 9 | 1 | 0 | 0 | 3 | 0 | 12 | 1 |
| 1938/39 | 26 | 0 | 4 | 0 | 1 | 0 | 31 | 0 |
| | 272 | 5 | 22 | 0 | 6 | 0 | 300 | 5 |

**Honours at Everton**
Division 1 winner: 1931/32, 1938/39
Division 2 winner: 1930/31
FA Cup winner: 1933
Caps for Scotland: 1

# ALEC TROUP

*Alec Troup was an abundantly talented winger, best known for his inch-perfect crosses.*

No decade in the twentieth century has produced more great flankmen than the 1920s. The Goodison crop of that era included Ted Critchley, George Harrison and Jimmy Stein, but arguably Troup was the most exhilarating of them all.

Troup had played for Forfar Athletic and Dundee before transferring to Everton for £1,950 in 1923. He was of slight build and overcame the inconvenience of a weak collarbone, which had to be heavily strapped before every game. This handicap did not inhibit his prowess as a spectacular dribbler and an accurate distributor of the ball. Troup enthralled the Goodison faithful by skipping past defenders and pin-pointing passes towards Dixie Dean. His perfectly-weighted crosses seemed to hang in the air waiting for the centre-forward's execution. Indeed, Dean was generous in his praise of the superior service from the left-winger and, predictably, it was from a beautifully-flighted corner by Troup that the legendary centre-forward headed his record-breaking sixtieth League goal in the final outing of the 1927/28 championship campaign.

Troup was capped by Scotland against England in 1926. But having lost his place in Everton's first-team to young Jimmy Stein, the diminutive outside-left returned to Dundee in early 1930. However, the transition was far from seamless. Everton struggled without Troup and, at the end of the dismal 1929/30 season, were relegated for the first-time in their illustrious history.

Born: Forfar, 1895
Height: 1.65 m (5 ft 5 in) Weight: 66.7 kg (10 st 7 lb)

| | League apps | League goals | FA Cup apps | FA Cup goals | Other apps | Other goals | Total apps | Total goals |
|---|---|---|---|---|---|---|---|---|
| 1922/23 | 17 | 2 | 0 | 0 | 0 | 0 | 17 | 2 |
| 1923/24 | 41 | 1 | 2 | 0 | 0 | 0 | 43 | 1 |
| 1924/25 | 32 | 2 | 0 | 0 | 0 | 0 | 32 | 2 |
| 1925/26 | 38 | 6 | 2 | 0 | 0 | 0 | 40 | 6 |
| 1926/27 | 37 | 5 | 4 | 2 | 0 | 0 | 41 | 7 |
| 1927/28 | 42 | 10 | 2 | 1 | 0 | 0 | 44 | 11 |
| 1928/29 | 38 | 5 | 0 | 0 | 1 | 0 | 39 | 5 |
| 1929/30 | 4 | 1 | 0 | 0 | 0 | 0 | 4 | 1 |
| | 249 | 32 | 10 | 3 | 1 | 0 | 260 | 35 |

**Honours at Everton**
Division 1 winner: 1927/28
Caps for Scotland: 1

# ROY VERNON

*Royston Vernon was an expert striker
with a shot of venomous power.*

Having bungled the opportunity to sign Vernon as a schoolboy, Everton did not hesitate to acquire his services the second time around in 1960. The part-exchange deal with Blackburn Rovers for the Wales international involved Eddie Thomas plus £27,000 moving to Ewood Park. At Everton, Vernon was hailed as a clinical striker and developed a fruitful understanding with Alex Young. He finished top scorer in each of his four full seasons at Goodison.

Vernon was extremely quick in short bursts and displayed an impressive array of magnetic ball skills, but by no stretch of the imagination did he resemble a professional athlete. The gifted inside-forward weighed in at only 62.8 kg, but his slight frame belied his toughness, tempestuous nature and courage. As a result of his whiplash reflexes and sharp-shooting, Vernon averaged 0.550 goals per game during his time at Everton. He was also respected as one of the finest strikers of the ball and an outstanding penalty-taker, converting 15 out of 16 spot-kicks.

Vernon captained Everton's assault on the 1962/63 League championship and made a significant contribution towards lifting the trophy, thereby ending a frustrating period of under-achievement at the club. He led by example and scored 24 League goals, including a hat-trick in the final game against Fulham. But after scrapes with the club management as well as the odd referee, Vernon was sold to Stoke City for £40,000 in 1965. He later played for Halifax Town. The Wales star also made his mark on the international stage and was awarded 32 caps, 13 of them at Everton.

Born: Ffynnongroew, Flintshire, 1937
Height: 1.73 m (5 ft 8 in)  Weight: 62.8 kg (9 st 12 lb)

|  | League | | FA Cup | | Other | | Europe | | Total | |
|---|---|---|---|---|---|---|---|---|---|---|
|  | apps | goals | apps | goals | apps | goals | apps | goals | apps | goals |
| 1959/60 | 12 | 9 | 0 | 0 | 0 | 0 | 0 | 0 | 12 | 9 |
| 1960/61 | 39 | 21 | 1 | 0 | 4 | 1 | 0 | 0 | 44 | 22 |
| 1961/62 | 37 | 26 | 3 | 2 | 0 | 0 | 0 | 0 | 40 | 28 |
| 1962/63 | 41 | 24 | 3 | 3 | 0 | 0 | 2 | 0 | 46 | 27 |
| 1963/64 | 31 | 18 | 5 | 2 | 1 | 1 | 2 | 0 | 39 | 21 |
| 1964/65 | 16 | 3 | 0 | 0 | 0 | 0 | 3 | 1 | 19 | 4 |
|  | 176 | 101 | 12 | 7 | 5 | 2 | 7 | 1 | 200 | 111 |

**Honours at Everton**
Division 1 winner: 1962/63
Caps for Wales: 13

# DAVE WATSON

*Dave Watson is a formidable defender
and one of Everton's greatest servants.*

Watson's transformation has been so complete that many fans believe that he was born in royal blue. In fact Watson kicked off his career with four Central League outings for Liverpool. Bought from Norwich City for a club record fee of £900,000, he has earned a well-deserved place in the hearts of the fans with his courageous displays. Watson is renowned for not embroidering his play with intricate touches and, as a result, most of his outings have been near-flawless.

Watson recently joined the 500-game elite and has been required to wear several hats during his Everton career, serving as club captain, caretaker-manager and player-coach. He was an important member of the Everton teams which carried off the Division 1 title in 1986/87 and dramatically won the 1995 FA Cup final. Watson received half a dozen international caps during his spell at Norwich City and gained another six caps with Everton, his final England appearance was against the USSR in 1986. He also holds the distinction of playing for Hong Kong Golden Select XI against England a decade later. Watson is the only member of the 1999 playing staff in Gwladys Street's Hall of Fame.

Born: Liverpool, 1961
Height: 1.85 m (6 ft 1 in) Weight: 76.7 kg (12 st 1 lb)

| | League | | FA Cup | | Other | | Europe | | Total | |
|---|---|---|---|---|---|---|---|---|---|---|
| | apps | goals | apps | goals | apps | goals | apps | goals | apps | goals |
| 1986/87 | 35 | 4 | 3 | 0 | 4 | 0 | 0 | 0 | 42 | 4 |
| 1987/88 | 37 | 4 | 8 | 1 | 9 | 1 | 0 | 0 | 54 | 6 |
| 1988/89 | 32 | 2 | 7 | 0 | 8 | 1 | 0 | 0 | 47 | 3 |
| 1989/90 | 28/1 | 1 | 4 | 0 | 3 | 0 | 0 | 0 | 35/1 | 1 |
| 1990/91 | 32 | 2 | 6 | 2 | 8 | 2 | 0 | 0 | 46 | 6 |
| 1991/92 | 35 | 3 | 2 | 0 | 6 | 1 | 0 | 0 | 43 | 4 |
| 1992/93 | 40 | 1 | 2 | 1 | 6 | 0 | 0 | 0 | 48 | 2 |
| 1993/94 | 27/1 | 1 | 0 | 0 | 3 | 3 | 0 | 0 | 30/1 | 4 |
| 1994/95 | 38 | 2 | 6 | 1 | 2 | 1 | 0 | 0 | 46 | 4 |
| 1995/96 | 34 | 1 | 4 | 0 | 1/1 | 0 | 2 | 0 | 41/1 | 1 |
| 1996/97 | 29 | 1 | 2 | 0 | 0 | 0 | 0 | 0 | 31 | 1 |
| 1997/98 | 25/1 | 1 | 0 | 0 | 3 | 0 | 0 | 0 | 28/1 | 1 |
| 1998/99 | 22 | 0 | 3 | 0 | 1 | 1 | 0 | 0 | 26 | 1 |
| *up to July 1999* | **414/3** | **23** | **47** | **5** | **54/1** | **10** | **2** | **0** | **517/4** | **38** |

**Honours at Everton**
Division 1 winner: 1986/87
FA Cup winner: 1995
FA Cup runner-up: 1989
Simod Cup runner-up: 1988/89
Zenith Data Systems Cup runner-up: 1990/91
Caps for England: 6

**Caretaker management record at Everton 1996/97**
League: 1 win, 3 draws, 3 defeats

# GORDON WATSON

*Gordon Watson dedicated the best years
of his life to the club.*

Thomas Gordon Watson joined Everton from Blyth Spartans in 1933. The complex deal involved another player named John Gordon Watson, but whereas the latter moved on to Coventry City within 12 months - the former spent 64 years with Everton.

Watson was widely acknowledged as one of the best passers of the ball in the pre-war game. The skilful wing-half was also considered a versatile footballer and was often selected as twelfth man for the first-team, spending most Saturdays on the trainer's bench. His devotion to duty was recognised by his team-mates who presented him with a royal blue cushion on his twenty-fifth birthday. He broke into the first-team line-up in 1938, replacing Jock Thomson, and contributed to the successful championship run-in. Watson retained his place for the start of the following season but the League programme was terminated after only three games.

Like many of his young team-mates, Watson's career was significantly impacted by World War II. He made 203 appearances for Everton in regional league and cup competitions and also played in 38 post-war games before hanging up his boots in 1948. Subsequently he joined the Everton coaching staff and supervised the development of young stars for two decades. Watson transferred to the promotions department and later served the club as barman, steward and stadium tour guide. The grand old man of Goodison retired at age 83 in 1997.

Born: Seghill, 1914
Height: 1.70 m (5 ft 7 in)  Weight: 66.7 kg (10 st 7 lb)

| | League | | FA Cup | | Other | | Total | |
|---|---|---|---|---|---|---|---|---|
| | apps | goals | apps | goals | apps | goals | apps | goals |
| 1936/37 | 2 | 0 | 0 | 0 | 0 | 0 | 2 | 0 |
| 1937/38 | 9 | 1 | 0 | 0 | 0 | 0 | 9 | 1 |
| 1938/39 | 16 | 0 | 1 | 0 | 0 | 0 | 17 | 0 |
| 1946/47 | 12 | 0 | 0 | 0 | 0 | 0 | 12 | 0 |
| 1947/48 | 18 | 0 | 4 | 0 | 0 | 0 | 22 | 0 |
| 1948/49 | 4 | 0 | 0 | 0 | 0 | 0 | 4 | 0 |
| | 61 | 1 | 5 | 0 | 0 | 0 | 66 | 1 |

**Honours at Everton**
Division 1 winner: 1938/39

# GORDON WEST

*Gordon West was an acrobatic goalkeeper
who cost a British record fee.*

Even though West had played only 31 League games for Blackpool, Everton manager Harry Catterick did not hesitate to sign the 18-year old for £27,500 in 1962. The young custodian had demonstrated tremendous acrobatic abilities during his brief stint at Bloomfield Road. He proved to be a tremendous signing and realised his rich potential by playing over 400 games in the top flight.

West was capable of hurling his massive frame to all corners of his goal with spectacular agility and also displayed breath-taking reflexes and reassuring dexterity in dealing with crosses. He also used his gigantic physique to make superlative one-on-one saves by narrowing angles with geometric precision and to launch attacks by throwing the ball beyond the half-way line. Like many of his predecessors, West established a tremendous rapport with Merseyside fans of all persuasions and, during his 12 seasons with the Toffees, won two League titles, the FA Cup and a few fashion accessories from his friends on the Kop. Although his abilities and consistency brought him to the attention of Sir Alf Ramsey, West's international outings were halted after he declined to be included in the 1970 World Cup squad. Not long afterwards, he started to suffer from pre-match nerves as well as occasional lapses in concentration and had to battle with Andy Rankin for the Everton No 1 spot. West retired in 1973 but some three years later embarked on a brief come-back with Tranmere Rovers.

Born: Barnsley, 1943
Height: 1.86 m (6 ft 1 in) Weight: 86.5 kg (13 st 9 lb)

| | League apps | League goals | FA Cup apps | FA Cup goals | Other apps | Other goals | Europe apps | Europe goals | Total apps | Total goals |
|---|---|---|---|---|---|---|---|---|---|---|
| 1961/62 | 12 | 0 | 0 | 0 | 0 | 0 | 0 | 0 | 12 | 0 |
| 1962/63 | 38 | 0 | 3 | 0 | 0 | 0 | 2 | 0 | 43 | 0 |
| 1963/64 | 22 | 0 | 3 | 0 | 1 | 0 | 2 | 0 | 28 | 0 |
| 1964/65 | 20 | 0 | 4 | 0 | 0 | 0 | 2 | 0 | 26 | 0 |
| 1965/66 | 24 | 0 | 8 | 0 | 0 | 0 | 2 | 0 | 34 | 0 |
| 1966/67 | 36 | 0 | 5 | 0 | 1 | 0 | 4 | 0 | 46 | 0 |
| 1967/68 | 41 | 0 | 6 | 0 | 2 | 0 | 0 | 0 | 49 | 0 |
| 1968/69 | 42 | 0 | 5 | 0 | 4 | 0 | 0 | 0 | 51 | 0 |
| 1969/70 | 42 | 0 | 1 | 0 | 4 | 0 | 0 | 0 | 47 | 0 |
| 1970/71 | 12 | 0 | 1 | 0 | 1 | 0 | 1 | 0 | 15 | 0 |
| 1971/72 | 42 | 0 | 4 | 0 | 1 | 0 | 0 | 0 | 47 | 0 |
| 1972/73 | 4 | 0 | 0 | 0 | 0 | 0 | 0 | 0 | 4 | 0 |
| | 335 | 0 | 40 | 0 | 14 | 0 | 13 | 0 | 402 | 0 |

**Honours at Everton**
Division 1 winner: 1962/63, 1969/70
FA Cup winner: 1966
FA Cup runner-up: 1968
Caps for England: 3
Caps for England Under-23: 2
Appearances for the Football League: 1

# TOMMY WHITE

*Tommy White gave a good account
of himself wherever he was asked to perform.*

Equipped with a growing reputation as a talented outside-right, White joined Everton from Southport for £1,000 in 1927. But as the youngster filled out, Everton deployed him in various different berths. Remarkably, the all-rounder performed with distinction at wing-half, inside forward, centre-forward and centre-half and also scored goals from most of these positions. But for the bulk of his career, White alternated between centre-half and centre-forward.

White's massive physique was key to his powerful style of play. As a pivot, he was a formidable tower of strength feared by opponents for his fierce tackling. Few forwards got the better of him and the rugged defender played an important part in the Toffees capturing the FA Cup in 1933. At the other end of the pitch, as a deputy for Dixie Dean, White developed into an intimidating spearhead and a very effective goal-poacher. He displayed determination and endeavour in copious quantities and was rewarded with 66 goals during his Goodison career. Irrespective of where he played, White was committed to doing his best for Everton.

White was capped by England at centre-half on one occasion, for the match against Italy in 1933. Towards the end of his career, he was required to contest the Everton centre-half position with England international Charlie Gee and Wales star TG Jones. He subsequently moved on to Northampton Town and then New Brighton. White died following a fall at Liverpool Docks in 1967, where he had worked after leaving football.

Born: Manchester, 1908
Height: 1.75 m (5 ft 9 in) Weight: 84.1 kg (13 st 3 lb)

|  | League | | FA Cup | | Other | | Total | |
|---|---|---|---|---|---|---|---|---|
|  | apps | goals | apps | goals | apps | goals | apps | goals |
| 1927/28 | 1 | 2 | 0 | 0 | 0 | 0 | 1 | 2 |
| 1928/29 | 21 | 6 | 0 | 0 | 0 | 0 | 21 | 6 |
| 1929/30 | 35 | 11 | 0 | 0 | 0 | 0 | 35 | 11 |
| 1930/31 | 10 | 10 | 0 | 0 | 0 | 0 | 10 | 10 |
| 1931/32 | 23 | 18 | 1 | 0 | 0 | 0 | 24 | 18 |
| 1932/33 | 34 | 2 | 6 | 0 | 1 | 0 | 41 | 2 |
| 1933/34 | 28 | 14 | 1 | 0 | 1 | 0 | 30 | 14 |
| 1934/35 | 5 | 0 | 0 | 0 | 0 | 0 | 5 | 0 |
| 1935/36 | 35 | 3 | 1 | 0 | 0 | 0 | 36 | 3 |
| 1936/37 | 1 | 0 | 0 | 0 | 0 | 0 | 1 | 0 |
|  | 193 | 66 | 9 | 0 | 2 | 0 | 204 | 66 |

**Honours at Everton**
Division 1 winner: 1931/32
Division 2 winner: 1930/31
FA Cup winner: 1933
Caps for England: 1

# RAY WILSON

*Ramon Wilson was perfection at No 3,
the best full-back to have played for Everton.*

Wilson had been groomed for stardom by Bill Shankly at Huddersfield Town and had made 266 League appearances with the Yorkshire-club and gained 30 England caps before joining Everton in 1964. The £40,000 transaction involved Eire international Mick Meagan moving to Leeds Road in exchange for the 30-year old full-back.

Befitting a world-class defender, Wilson was an astute tactician and intelligent reader of the game. His other impeccable credentials included blistering pace in short bursts, great finesse with the ball and confidence under pressure. Within no time at all, the elegant left-back gained unilateral admiration with his exquisite exhibitions of adroit defending and menacing overlapping.

He helped bring the FA Cup to Everton after an absence of 33 years, but perhaps Wilson is best remembered for his significant contributions towards England capturing the Jules Rimet trophy in 1966. He was the only Everton participant in the England team at the time of the World Cup and his performances in the tournament reinforced his world-class standing.

Disappointingly, Wilson made only 154 appearances for the club. His outings for Everton and England were cut short by a knee injury. He was transferred to Oldham Athletic in 1969 and joined Bradford City as player-coach the following season. Wilson retired from football to become the nation's most-famous undertaker.

Born: Shirebrook, 1934
Height: 1.73m (5 ft 8 in) Weight: 66.7 kg (10 st 7 lb)

|  | League apps | League goals | FA Cup apps | FA Cup goals | Other apps | Other goals | Europe apps | Europe goals | Total apps | Total goals |
|---|---|---|---|---|---|---|---|---|---|---|
| 1964/65 | 17 | 0 | 4 | 0 | 0 | 0 | 2 | 0 | 23 | 0 |
| 1965/66 | 35 | 0 | 8 | 0 | 0 | 0 | 4 | 0 | 47 | 0 |
| 1966/67 | 30 | 0 | 6 | 0 | 1 | 0 | 4 | 0 | 41 | 0 |
| 1967/68 | 28 | 0 | 6 | 0 | 0 | 0 | 0 | 0 | 34 | 0 |
| 1968/69 | 4/2 | 0 | 2 | 0 | 0/1 | 0 | 0 | 0 | 6/3 | 0 |
|  | 114/2 | 0 | 26 | 0 | 1/1 | 0 | 10 | 0 | 151/3 | 0 |

**Honours at Everton**
FA Cup winner: 1966
FA Cup runner-up: 1968
Caps for England: 33
World Cup winner: 1966
Appearances for the Football League: 3

# TOMMY WRIGHT

*Tommy Wright was a top-class defender
and a dedicated club-man.*

Shortly after Wright pledged himself to Everton in 1963, the apprentice inside-forward was converted into a top-notch right-back. His youthful promise was confirmed when he made his senior debut twelve months later. Subsequently he monopolised the right-back position for the best part of a decade and made 373 first-team appearances for the club.

The thoroughbred full-back was fleet of foot and liked to mix his defensive duties with enterprising surges along the touch-line. But there was much more to his game than pace and fitness. He possessed a sharp football brain and, as a result, was quick to sense danger, deny space to opponents and either move into tackle or execute shrewd interceptions. In addition, the England international demonstrated comfort on the ball and tactical awareness to develop a productive rearguard understanding with Everton and England team-mate Ray Wilson.

Wright was a formidable member of the Everton teams which won the Division 1 crown and the FA Cup in the 1960s. His club performances were rewarded with 11 England caps and he responded by blossoming in the 1970 World Cup sunshine in Mexico, where England were unfortunate not to retain the Jules Rimet trophy. Ironically throughout the tournament, he was required to contest the England right-back spot with Keith Newton, his new Goodison partner. Injury forced Wright out of the game at the age of 29, when he was still at his peak. His premature retirement was a bitter blow for the player and his club.

Born: Liverpool, 1944
Height: 1.73 m (5 ft 8 in)  Weight: 71.3 kg (11 st 3 lb)

| | League | | FA Cup | | Other | | Europe | | Total | |
|---|---|---|---|---|---|---|---|---|---|---|
| | apps | goals | apps | goals | apps | goals | apps | goals | apps | goals |
| 1964/65 | 22 | 0 | 3 | 0 | 0 | 0 | 3 | 0 | 28 | 0 |
| 1965/66 | 35/1 | 0 | 6 | 0 | 0 | 0 | 4 | 0 | 45/1 | 0 |
| 1966/67 | 42 | 0 | 6 | 0 | 1 | 0 | 4 | 0 | 53 | 0 |
| 1967/68 | 38 | 0 | 6 | 0 | 2 | 0 | 0 | 0 | 46 | 0 |
| 1968/69 | 41 | 1 | 5 | 0 | 4 | 0 | 0 | 0 | 50 | 1 |
| 1969/70 | 42 | 1 | 1 | 0 | 4 | 0 | 0 | 0 | 47 | 1 |
| 1970/71 | 40 | 2 | 5 | 0 | 1 | 0 | 6 | 0 | 52 | 2 |
| 1971/72 | 17 | 0 | 1 | 0 | 0 | 0 | 0 | 0 | 18 | 0 |
| 1972/73 | 30 | 0 | 2 | 0 | 1 | 0 | 0 | 0 | 33 | 0 |
| | 307/1 | 4 | 35 | 0 | 13 | 0 | 17 | 0 | 372/1 | 4 |

**Honours at Everton**
Division 1 winner: 1969/70
FA Cup winner: 1966
FA Cup runner-up: 1968
Caps for England: 11
Caps for England Under-23: 7

# ALEX YOUNG

*Alex Young was 'The Golden Vision',*
*one of the most graceful footballers of all time.*

Young launched his career with Heart of Midlothian and, with the football world at his feet, was enticed away from the reigning Scottish League champions by Everton manager Johnny Carey. The £55,000 package also included full-back George Thomson moving to Merseyside. Young was valued at £42,000. Once settled at his new home, the Scotland centre-forward was a revelation. He helped Everton to capture the 1962/63 League championship as well as the 1966 FA Cup and became the beloved idol of the Gwladys Street terraces.

Young found Goodison Park to be the ideal stage for his silky skills. Although plagued by blistered feet throughout his career, the god-like centre-forward led the line with breath-taking footwork. He bewildered opponents with his magical dribbling skills, pirouetted from challenges and glided across the pitch to seduce the Goodison faithful. His game was a collage of graceful first-touches, deft back-heels, delicate feints, elegant body swerves and hallmarked goals.

Probably the most idolised footballer of his generation, Young inspired a 1968 television drama written by Neville Smith. But hero-worship did not emanate from Harry Catterick and the fans' favourite engaged in a titanic battle of personalities with the Everton manager. As a result, Young abdicated to Glentoran as player-manager in 1968. He returned briefly to English football with Stockport County in Division 3 and played out the remainder of the 1968/69 season before retiring. But three decades later 'The Golden Vision' exerts an almost mythical appeal among those of the royal blue persuasion and other connoisseurs of entertaining football.

Born: Loanhead, 1937
Height: 1.73 m (5 ft 8 in) Weight: 68.0 kg (10 st 10 lb)

| | League apps | League goals | FA Cup apps | FA Cup goals | Other apps | Other goals | Europe apps | Europe goals | Total apps | Total goals |
|---|---|---|---|---|---|---|---|---|---|---|
| 1960/61 | 13 | 6 | 0 | 0 | 1 | 1 | 0 | 0 | 14 | 7 |
| 1961/62 | 40 | 14 | 3 | 0 | 0 | 0 | 0 | 0 | 43 | 14 |
| 1962/63 | 42 | 22 | 3 | 0 | 0 | 0 | 2 | 0 | 47 | 22 |
| 1963/64 | 27 | 12 | 3 | 0 | 1 | 0 | 2 | 0 | 33 | 12 |
| 1964/65 | 20 | 3 | 1 | 0 | 0 | 0 | 3 | 3 | 24 | 6 |
| 1965/66 | 26 | 7 | 8 | 2 | 0 | 0 | 2 | 0 | 36 | 9 |
| 1966/67 | 35 | 8 | 5 | 2 | 1 | 0 | 4 | 0 | 45 | 10 |
| 1967/68 | 24/1 | 5 | 2/2 | 0 | 2 | 2 | 0 | 0 | 28/3 | 7 |
| | 227/1 | 77 | 25/2 | 4 | 5 | 3 | 13 | 3 | 270/3 | 87 |

**Honours at Everton**
Division 1 winner: 1962/63
FA Cup winner: 1966
Caps for Scotland: 2

# SANDY YOUNG

*Alex 'Sandy' Young scored the goal
that brought the English Cup to Merseyside.*

Young polished his skills with St Mirren and Falkirk before moving to Goodison for £100. He was a potent hit-man and scored 125 goals during his decade with the club. But none of his goals was as important as his strike in the seventy-fifth minute of the 1906 English Cup final when he coolly diverted a cross from Jack Sharp past Aitken, the Newcastle United custodian. Surprisingly the centre-forward's firepower failed to capture any more trophies, even though the Toffees came very close to earning League championship honours in 1901/02, 1904/05 and 1908/09.

Like his namesake from a later era, the stylish centre-forward relied on cleverness and artistic footwork to master more physically imposing opponents and suffered from the occasional tendency to over-elaborate. He was a splendid dribbler, often leading opponents a merry dance. Although Young was troubled by periods of ill-health during his Goodison career, when fully fit he was arguably one of the finest centre-forwards in the land.

Young was awarded two international caps by Scotland before moving on to Tottenham Hotspur in 1911. He returned to the North West for spells with Manchester City and South Liverpool before emigrating to Australia in 1914. The following year, Young was charged with the wilful murder of his brother and was found guilty of manslaughter.

Born: Slamannan, 1880
Height: 1.75 m (5 ft 9 in)  Weight: 70.8 kg (11 st 2 lb)

|  | League | | FA Cup | | Total | |
|---|---|---|---|---|---|---|
|  | apps | goals | apps | goals | apps | goals |
| 1901/02 | 30 | 6 | 2 | 1 | 32 | 7 |
| 1902/03 | 19 | 5 | 1 | 0 | 20 | 5 |
| 1903/04 | 22 | 10 | 0 | 0 | 22 | 10 |
| 1904/05 | 31 | 14 | 6 | 0 | 37 | 14 |
| 1905/06 | 30 | 12 | 5 | 2 | 35 | 14 |
| 1906/07 | 33 | 28 | 8 | 1 | 41 | 29 |
| 1907/08 | 33 | 16 | 6 | 5 | 39 | 21 |
| 1908/09 | 23 | 9 | 1 | 0 | 24 | 9 |
| 1909/10 | 24 | 2 | 7 | 3 | 31 | 5 |
| 1910/11 | 30 | 8 | 3 | 3 | 33 | 11 |
|  | 275 | 110 | 39 | 15 | 314 | 125 |

**Honours at Everton**
Division 1 runner-up: 1901/02, 1904/05, 1908/09
FA Cup (English Cup) winner: 1906
FA Cup (English Cup) runner-up: 1907
Caps for Scotland: 2

# 1999

## GWLADYS STREET'S HALL OF FAME

Walter Abbott

John Bell

Cliff Britton

Bobby Collins

Dixie Dean

Wally Fielding

Fred Geary

Harold Hardman

Adrian Heath

Tommy Jones

Andy King

Tommy Lawton

Joe Mercer

Alex Parker

Peter Reid

Jimmy Settle

Neville Southall

Gary Stevens

Jock Thomson

Gordon Watson

Tommy Wright

Alan Ball

Billy Bingham

Harry Catterick

Billy Cook

Jimmy Dunn

Tom Fleetwood

Charlie Gee

Brian Harris

Dave Hickson

TG Jones

Brian Labone

Mike Lyons

Alf Milward

Bobby Parker

Joe Royle

Graeme Sharp

Jack Southworth

Alex Stevenson

Alec Troup

Gordon West

Alex Young

Billy Balmer

Richard Boyle

Edgar Chadwick

Warney Cresswell

Tommy Eglington

Bertie Freeman

Albert Geldard

Hunter Hart

Johnny Holt

Howard Kendall

Bob Latchford

George Mahon

John Moores

John Willie Parker

Ted Sagar

Jack Sharp

Jimmy Stein

Jack Taylor

Roy Vernon

Tommy White

Sandy Young

James Baxter

Paul Bracewell

Sam Chedgzoy

Will Cuff

Peter Farrell

Jimmy Gabriel

Andy Gray

Colin Harvey

John Hurst

Roger Kenyon

Alex Latta

Harry Makepeace

Johnny Morrissey

Kevin Ratcliffe

Billy Scott

Kevin Sheedy

Trevor Steven

Derek Temple

Dave Watson

Ray Wilson

WALTER ABBOTT

BILLY BALMER

JAMES BAXTER

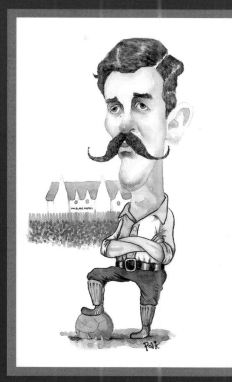

JOHN BELL

BILLY BINGHAM

RICHARD BOYLE

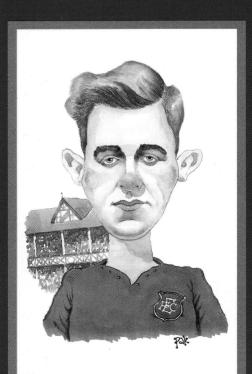

CLIFF BRITTON

HARRY CATTERICK

ALAN BALL

EDGAR CHADWICK

SAM CHEDGZOY

BOBBY COLLINS

BILLY COOK

PAUL BRACEWELL

WILL CUFF

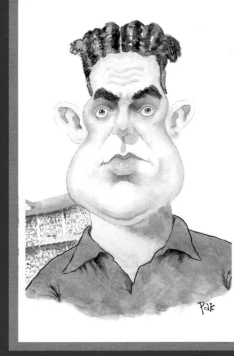

DIXIE DEAN

JIMMY DUNN

PETER FARRELL

WARNEY CRESSWELL

**WALLY FIELDING**

**TOM FLEETWOOD**

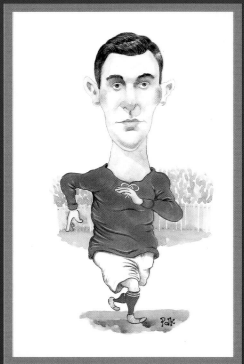

**BERTIE FREEMAN**

**JIMMY GABRIEL**

TOMMY EGLINGTON

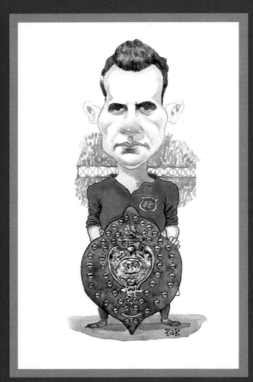

CHARLIE GEE

ALBERT GELDARD

ANDY GRAY

HAROLD HARDMAN

FRED GEARY

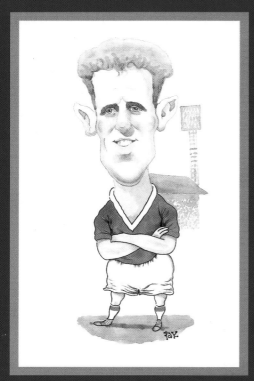

BRIAN HARRIS

HUNTER HART

ADRIAN HEATH

DAVE HICKSON

COLIN HARVEY

JOHNNY HOLT

JOHN HURST

TOMMY JONES

TG JONES

HOWARD KENDALL

ROGER KENYON

BRIAN LABONE

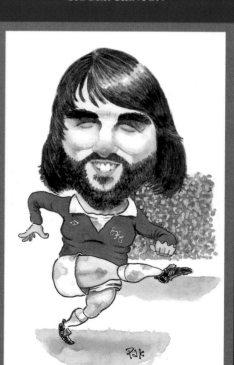

BOB LATCHFORD

ALEX LATTA

ANDY KING

TOMMY LAWTON

MIKE LYONS

GEORGE MAHON

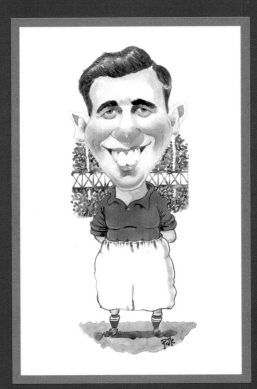

JOE MERCER

HARRY MAKEPEACE

ALF MILWARD

JOHN MOORES

JOHNNY MORRISSEY

ALEX PARKER

TED SAGAR

BOBBY PARKER

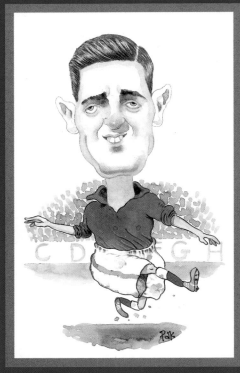

JOHN WILLIE PARKER

KEVIN RATCLIFFE

JOE ROYLE

PETER REID

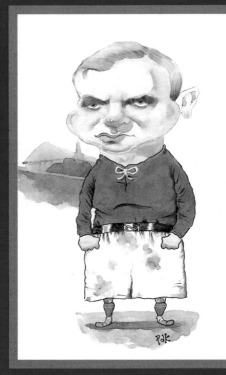

BILLY SCOTT

JIMMY SETTLE

GRAEME SHARP

JACK SHARP

NEVILLE SOUTHALL

KEVIN SHEEDY

JACK SOUTHWORTH

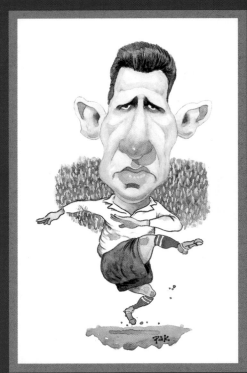

JIMMY STEIN

TREVOR STEVEN

JACK TAYLOR

GARY STEVENS

ALEX STEVENSON

DEREK TEMPLE

JOCK THOMSON

GORDON WATSON

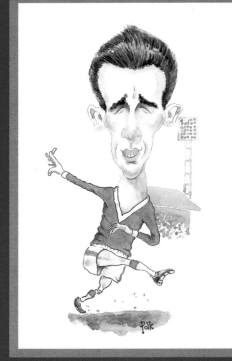

ALEC TROUP

ROY VERNON

DAVE WATSON

GORDON WEST

ALEX YOUNG

TOMMY WHITE

RAY WILSON

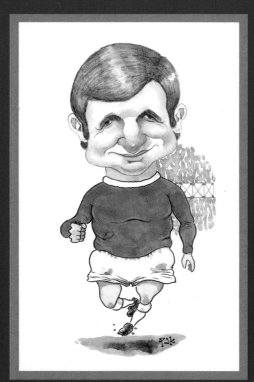

TOMMY WRIGHT

SANDY YOUNG

# ONLY THE BEST

New members will be added in future years but, by definition, only the best. will be good enough to be enshrined in Gwladys Street's Hall of Fame.

The short-list of candidates proposed for consideration in 2000 includes:

☆ Stan Bentham
☆ Sir Philip Carter
☆ Gary Lineker
☆ Duncan McKenzie
☆ Derek Mountfield
☆ Alex Scott

OTHERS

BLUE BLOODS

### STAN BENTHAM

After only a handful of games with non-League Wigan Athletic, Bentham was signed to play alongside Dean and subsequently Lawton. He was a hard-working inside-right and one of the unsung heroes of the 1938/39 championship team. His playing career at Everton spanned 15 seasons and included 211 outings and 53 goals in regional football during World War II. Bentham was also a member of the coaching staff for 14 seasons.

Everton: 125 appearances, 17 goals

## JOHN BAILEY

The stylish left-back was signed by manager Gordon Lee from Blackburn Rovers for £300,000 in 1979. Bailey made significant contributions to the 1984 FA Cup victory and 1984/85 League championship and was awarded one England 'B' international cap. He was renowned as a joker capable of lifting spirits in times of adversity. However, shortly after the arrival of the more robust Pat Van den Hauwe, Bailey was sold to Newcastle United for £80,000. He later moved to Bristol City and returned to Everton for a brief spell on the coaching staff in 1992.

Everton: 220/2 appearances, 3 goals

## PETER BEARDSLEY

Signed from Anfield for £1.0 million, the veteran England star was another of Howard Kendall's astute acquisitions. Previously with Carlisle United, Vancouver Whitecaps, Manchester United and Newcastle United, Beardsley had been one of the most talented footballers of his generation. He seemed to excel in operating behind the main strikers and converted the Goodison sceptics with his spectacular dribbling and razor-sharp marksmanship. However after only two seasons at Goodison, he moved back to Newcastle United for £1.4 million in 1993 and later played for Bolton Wanderers, Manchester City, Fulham and Hartlepool United.

Everton: 95 appearances, 32 goals

## Mr HARRY COOKE

Cooke understudied Jimmy Settle during the 1906 FA Cup run and was twelfth man for the final. After his playing days had been truncated by injury, Cooke joined the Everton backroom staff and made significant inputs to pre-match preparations and tactics for over three decades. The club trainer was also diligent in attending to the various aches, pains and injuries and nursed generations of Everton players back to fitness - his favourite patient was Dixie Dean. The dedicated club servant retired in 1961.

Everton: 9 appearances, 3 goals

## TONY COTTEE

A British record fee of £2.3 million lured Cottee from West Ham United in 1988. Nicknamed 'TC', he was blessed with strength, pace and astute positional sense. Cottee kicked off his Everton career with a hat-trick against Newcastle United and was the club's leading scorer for five of his six seasons at Goodison. However, the England striker failed to realise his full potential and was traded back to Upton Park in exchange for David Burrows. He continued to score goals for Selangor (Malaysia), Birmingham City and Leicester City.

Everton: 122/28 appearances, 55 goals

### Sir PHILIP CARTER

Carter was elected an Everton director in 1975 and served as club chairman during the glory years of the 1980s. His faith in Howard Kendall's management was rewarded with the European Cup-Winners' Cup, two Division 1 crowns and four FA Cup final appearances. He also served as president of the Football League.

Everton record during term as director/chairman (up to July 1999)

League: 386 wins, 280 draws, 322 defeats

## JACKIE COULTER

Belfast-born Coulter had spells with Cliftonville and Belfast Celtic before moving to Goodison for £3,000 in 1934. The outside-left exhibited teasing touch-line artistry, electrifying pace and an eye for goal. Coulter was a showman who liked to torment defenders and, as a result, was adored by the Everton fans. He earned five Northern Ireland caps but his football career was effectively ended when he suffered a fractured leg playing against Wales in 1937. He never fully recovered but went on to serve Grimsby Town, Swansea Town and Chelmsford.

Everton: 58 appearances, 24 goals

## TED CRITCHLEY

The fast and tricky right-winger was signed from Stockport County for £2,750 in 1926. During the next eight seasons, he won a host of admirers by providing pin-point crosses for Dixie Dean's execution. Critchley was a vital member of the Everton teams which earned two Division 1 titles as well as promotion from Division 2. Although the flankman grabbed the winning goal in the 1933 FA Cup semi-final, he was omitted for the Wembley showdown against Manchester City. Not long afterwards he left for Preston North End.

Everton: 230 appearances, 42 goals

## OLIVIER DACOURT

The fiery Frenchman was signed by manager Walter Smith from RC Strasbourg for £3.8 million. Previously capped by his country at Under-21 and 'B' levels, Dacourt combined crisp passing with abrasive tackling and stood out in a struggling Everton team. Although his uncompromising approach was embraced by the Goodison fans, the mid-fielder did not endear himself to referees. Dacourt always gave better than he took and received 11 yellow cards and one red card for his troubles. He was sold to Lens (France) for around £6.0 million at the end of one of the most fraught seasons in Everton's history.

Everton: 34/2 appearances, 3 goals

## DUNCAN FERGUSON

Ferguson kicked off his career with Dundee United and Glasgow Rangers. He was pried away from Ibrox by Mike Walker for a three-month loan spell and his £4.4 million transfer was completed by new manager Joe Royle in 1994. Ferguson's progress was interrupted by a catalogue of injuries, disciplinary problems and a 44-day spell in Barlinnie Prison. The towering centre-forward was feared for his aerial power as well as his deft footwork. He collected an FA Cup winners' medal in 1995 and was idolised in a manner enjoyed by few Premiership stars before his transfer to Newcastle United in 1998.

Everton: 133 appearances, 42 goals

**GARY LINEKER**

Lineker was signed from Leicester City for £800,000in 1985. Despite his prolific marksmanship, the Toffees failed to clinch the League and Cup double . After gaining personal honours including PFA 'Players' Player', PFW 'Footballer of the Year' and 11 England caps, he defected to Barcelona (Spain) for £2.5 million. Lineker reinforced his reputation with Tottenham Hotspur before joining Grampus Eight (Japan).

Everton: 57 appearances, 40 goals

## TORRY GILLICK

Gillick was signed from Glasgow Rangers for a record fee of £8,000 in 1935. The young winger was a natural crowd-pleaser and his dazzling footwork set up many goals in the 1938/39 League triumph. Like many of his team-mates, Gillick was denied further success by the outbreak of World War II. He guested for Aidrieonians and Glasgow Rangers in war-time football and returned to Ibrox in 1945, where he subsequently won Scottish League, Scottish Cup and Scottish League Cup medals. Gillick closed out his career with Partick Thistle.

Everton: 133 appearances, 44 goals

## ALAN HARPER

Signed by Howard Kendall from Liverpool, the versatile utility player repaid the £100,000 investment many times over. A model professional and one of the unsung heroes of the club's success in the 1980s, Harper filled most defensive and mid-field roles and also made 42 appearances as substitute before joining Sheffield Wednesday for £275,000 in 1988. Three years later, with the re-appointment of Kendall as Everton manager, he moved back to Goodison from Manchester City. Harper wound down his career with spells at Luton Town, Burnley and Cardiff City.

Everton: 194/42 appearances, 5 goals

## VAL HARRIS

Harris was hailed as the super-star of the Emerald Isle before joining Everton from Shelbourne in 1907. The Ireland international was respected for his astute football brain and perceptive passing and his impressive portfolio of skills made him a highly-valued utility player. The majority of his appearances were at right-half but he featured in four other positions at Everton. Despite his valiant efforts, Everton finished Division 1 runners-up on two occasions but won no major honours. However, He gained 14 of his 20 international caps during his stay on Merseyside before returning to Shelbourne in 1914.

Everton: 214 appearances, 2 goals

## BARRY HORNE

Previously with Rhyl, Wrexham and Portsmouth, Horne was signed from Southampton for a £675,000 fee set by a tribunal in 1992. He was a combative ball-winner - famed as a member of the 'Dogs of War' who captured the FA Cup in 1995. But perhaps Horne is best remembered for his spectacular equaliser against Wimbledon which helped Everton to retain their Premier League status in the final fixture of the 1993/94 season. The Wales international later served Birmingham City and Huddersfield Town and also came close to returning to Goodison in 1997.

Everton: 144/7 appearances, 3 goals

### DUNCAN McKENZIE

McKenzie was signed by manager Billy Bingham from Anderlecht (Belgium) for
£200,000 to partner Bob Latchford.  His dazzling footwork and flamboyant body-
swerves made him one of the most popular entertainers of the post-war era.  However,
he was discarded by new manager Gordon Lee in 1978.  His repertoire of skills took
him to Chelsea and Blackburn as well as the United States and Hong Kong.

Everton:  62 appearances,  21 goals

## JIMMY HUSBAND

A star of the victorious 1965 FA Youth Cup team, Husband was famed for his devastating pace. He paralysed defences with his unorthodox diagonal runs and dovetailed with Joe Royle to form the most exciting young strike force in the country. Although Husband was an influential member of the 1969/70 championship side, his progress was disrupted by injury and he subsequently struggled to hold down a first-team place. The England Under-23 international was sold to Luton Town in 1973 and later played for Memphis Rouges (USA).

Everton: 190/8 appearances, 55 goals

## BOBBY IRVINE

Signed from Dunmurry of the Irish Intermediate League for £500 in 1921, Irvine was well-equipped to play at either centre-forward or inside-right. The Ireland international mesmerised opponents with his tremendous dribbling skills and was awarded 11 caps during his Goodison career which spanned seven seasons. He was Dixie Dean's first side-kick and was a firm favourite with the royal blue fans. With the introduction of George Martin in 1928, he was sold to Portsmouth - part way through Everton's successful challenge for the League championship.

Everton: 214 appearances, 57 goals

## FRANK JEFFERIS

Discovered by Fordingbridge Turks and nurtured by Southampton in the Southern League, Jefferis moved to Merseyside for £750 in 1911. Best known as a scheming inside-forward, his subtle ball control and precise passing dismantled most defences. Along with Harry Makepeace, he was the driving force in the Everton engine room during the early part of the 1914/15 championship triumph. Jefferis collected two England caps and moved to Preston North End after World War I. He also served Southport as a player and a coach before joining Millwall's training staff.

Everton: 137 appearances, 25 goals

## TOMMY JOHNSON

'Tosh' Johnson had established goal-scoring records at Manchester City before joining Everton for £6,250 to aid the fight for survival in 1930. But despite his efforts, Everton were relegated for the first time in their history. Johnson was a gifted inside-left and responded by grabbing numerous important goals as Everton captured the Division 2 title, Division 1 championship and FA Cup in consecutive seasons. But shortly after losing his first-team place to Alex Stevenson in 1934, he moved on to Liverpool for £650.

Everton: 161 appearances, 65 goals

**DEREK MOUNTFIELD**

The life-long Evertonian was signed from Tranmere Rovers for £30,000 and matured into an influential member of the back-line which enjoyed domestic and European successes in the 1980s. Mountfield also exhibited an uncanny instinct for poaching goals. Capped by England at Under-21 and 'B' levels, he joined Aston Villa in 1986 and later played for Wolverhampton Wanderers, Carlisle United, Northampton Town and Walsall.

Everton: 152 appearances, 24 goals

### ANDREI KANCHELSKIS

Kanchelskis was signed by manager Joe Royle in 1995 for a club record fee of £5.0 million. Despite the transfer being mired by a dispute between his former clubs, Manchester United and Shaktyor Donetsk (USSR), the Ukrainian wide-boy was a revelation and lit up Goodison Park with exhilarating wing displays and stunning marksmanship. Kanchelskis suffered an inexplicable loss of form in early-1997 and was traded to Fiorentina (Italy) for £8.0 million. He joined Glasgow Rangers in 1998. The native of Kirovograd (Ukraine) was awarded international caps by the USSR, the CIS and Russia.

Everton: 60 appearances, 22 goals

### TONY KAY

The 25-year old hard-man was signed by manager Harry Catterick from Sheffield Wednesday for a record fee of £60,000 in 1962. Kay imposed himself on matches and was feared for his perceptive passes as much as his pulverising tackles. His arrival insured that the Toffees clinched the 1962/63 title. But sadly Everton were denied his long-term services after his match-fixing trial in 1965. Kay was jailed for four months and banned from football for life. The England star had allegedly wagered on Sheffield Wednesday losing at Ipswich shortly before his move to Goodison.

Everton: 58 appearances, 4 goals

### Mr THEO KELLY

Kelly was appointed club secretary after the death of Tom McIntosh and was elevated to Everton's first manager-secretary at the end of the successful 1938/39 campaign. His first seven years in the newly-created position embraced the difficulties of war-time regional football. However with the resumption of the Football League programme, Everton's results were less impressive and Kelly reverted to his former role. Although respected for his administrative acumen, he was far from popular with some players and was credited by his critics with orchestrating the departures of Dean, Lawton and Mercer.

Everton record during term as manager-secretary
League: 34 wins, 15 draws, 35 defeats

### FRED PICKERING

Pickering was signed from Blackburn Rovers for a club record fee of £85,000 in 1964. The rumbustious centre-forward matured into an accomplished marksman with a scorching right-foot shot. He netted hat-tricks on his debuts for Everton and England. Unfortunately, Pickering suffered a knee injury and after several lacklustre displays was axed from the 1966 FA Cup final line-up. Shortly afterwards he was transferred to Birmingham City for £50,000 and also played for Blackpool and Blackburn Rovers.

Everton: 115 appearances, 70 goals

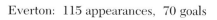

**ALEX SCOTT**

Previously with Camelon Thistle and Bo'ness United, Scott was signed from Glasgow
Rangers for £40,000 in 1963.  Known as 'Chico' to the fans, his devastating acceleration
reaped immediate rewards as Everton lifted the 1962/63 Division 1 title.  Scott also
starred in the 1966 FA Cup triumph before moving on to Hibernian for £15,000.
He gained five of his 16 Scotland caps during his stay at Goodison.

Everton:  176 appearances,  26 goals

## TOMMY RING

The 29-year old veteran was signed from Clyde for £8,000 in 1960. Ring made an immediate impact with the Goodison fans and was considered by many to have been the most gifted winger to have played for Everton in the post-war era. He was respected for his sublime ball skills and his ability to ghost past defenders and make pin-point accurate crosses. Sadly, Ring broke his leg at Stamford Bridge in 1960 and never played top-flight football again. He moved to Barnsley for £2,000 in 1961 and later had brief spells with Aberdeen, Fraserburgh and Stevenage Town.

Everton: 27 appearances, 6 goals

## DENNIS STEVENS

A cousin of Old Trafford legend Duncan Edwards, Stevens had helped Bolton Wanderers win the FA Cup in 1958. His arrival at Goodison for £35,000 four years later accelerated the departure of Bobby Collins to Leeds. Stevens proved to be a valuable recruit with an abundance of stamina, courage and skill. His tireless and unselfish efforts made him one of the unsung heroes of the 1962/63 League championship team. However with the rapid development of Colin Harvey, he moved on to Oldham Athletic for £20,000. Stevens later played for Tranmere Rovers.

Everton: 142 appearances, 22 goals

## GRAHAM STUART

Snapped up from Chelsea for £850,000 during Howard Kendall's second spell in the Everton hot-seat, Stuart was a hard-working footballer who could play up-front or forage in mid-field. He also scored one of the most important goals in the club's history - his second strike in the 1994 relegation dog-fight with Wimbledon slipped past Hans Segers to keep Everton in the Premier League. Stuart was an integral part of the 1995 FA Cup winning team but three seasons later was traded to Sheffield United in an exchange deal involving Carl Tiler and Mitch Ward. He later moved to Charlton Athletic.

Everton: 137/24 appearances, 31 goals

## ALAN WHITTLE

Whittle rocketed to prominence in the second half of the 1969/70 title race as a 19 year-old deputy for Jimmy Husband. He netted several vital away goals and his overall tally of 11 goals in 15 outings was a revelation. Whittle's sense of time and space as well as his instinctive feet made him a lethal finisher and he was heralded as the greatest discovery of all time by manager Harry Catterick. However his star faded and, after bouts of indifferent form, he was sold to Crystal Palace for £100,000 in 1972. The England Under-23 forward later played for Leyton Orient and Bournemouth.

Everton: 83/6 appearances, 26 goals

Football is a game of opinions! Inputs pertaining to various fields of endeavour were solicited from a cross-section of Everton enthusiasts ...

| | GOLDEN OLDIES |
|---|---|
| 1 | Ted Sagar |
| 2 | Wally Fielding |
| 3 | Neville Southall |
| 4 | Dave Watson |
| 5 | Richard Gough |
| 6 | Alex Stevenson |
| 7 | Howard Kendall |
| 8 | Peter Farrell |
| 9 | Kenny Samson |
| 10 | Ray Wilson |
| 11 | Jim Arnold |
| 12 | Kevin Sheedy |

| | POWERFUL HEADERS |
|---|---|
| 1 | Brian Labone |
| 2 | Duncan Ferguson |
| 3 | Joe Royle |
| 4 | TG Jones |
| 5 | Andy Gray |
| 6 | Bob Latchford |
| 7 | Alex Young |
| 8 | Dave Watson |
| 9 | Mark Higgins |
| 10 | Dave Hickson |
| 11 | Graeme Sharp |
| 12 | Frank Wignall |

| | EXPLOSIVE KICKERS |
|---|---|
| 1 | Roy Vernon |
| 2 | Fred Pickering |
| 3 | Bruce Rioch |
| 4 | Sandy Brown |
| 5 | Joe Royle |
| 6 | Graeme Sharp |
| 7 | Kevin Sheedy |
| 8 | Bobby Collins |
| 9 | Derek Temple |
| 10 | Dave Hickson |
| 11 | Bob Latchford |
| 12 | Andy Hinchcliffe |

| | CLASSY DEFENDERS |
|---|---|
| 1 | TG Jones |
| 2 | Ray Wilson |
| 3 | Brian Labone |
| 4 | Colin Todd |
| 5 | Keith Newton |
| 6 | Alex Parker |
| 7 | Ian Snodin |
| 8 | John Hurst |
| 9 | Marco Materazzi |
| 10 | Tommy Wright |
| 11 | John Gidman |
| 12 | John Bailey |

| | MID-FIELD DYNAMOS |
|---|---|
| 1 | Alan Ball |
| 2 | Colin Harvey |
| 3 | Peter Reid |
| 4 | Howard Kendall |
| 5 | Asa Hartford |
| 6 | Bobby Collins |
| 7 | Paul Bracewell |
| 8 | Mick Buckley |
| 9 | Jimmy Gabriel |
| 10 | Peter Farrell |
| 11 | Steve McMahon |
| 12 | Andy King |

| | TOUGH GUYS |
|---|---|
| 1 | Tony Kay |
| 2 | Johnny Morrissey |
| 3 | Roger Kenyon |
| 4 | Bobby Collins |
| 5 | Bruce Rioch |
| 6 | Mick Bernard |
| 7 | Mike Pejic |
| 8 | Kevin Ratcliffe |
| 9 | Duncan Ferguson |
| 10 | Pat Van den Hauwe |
| 11 | Dave Watson |
| 12 | David Unsworth |

| | MOST CELEBRATED POST-WAR GOALS | | |
|---|---|---|---|
| 1 | Graeme Sharp | October 20, 1984 | Liverpool |
| 2 | Graham Stuart | May 7, 1994 | Wimbledon (No 2) |
| 3 | Derek Temple | May 15, 1966 | Sheffield Wednesday |
| 4 | Gareth Farrelly | May 10, 1998 | Coventry City |
| 5 | Alan Ball | March 11, 1967 | Liverpool |
| 6 | Paul Rideout | May 20, 1995 | Manchester United |
| 7 | Andy Gray | April 24, 1985 | Bayern Munich |
| 8 | Alex Young | April 20, 1963 | Tottenham Hotspur |
| 9 | Andy King | October 28, 1978 | Liverpool |
| 10 | Adrian Heath | January 18, 1984 | Oxford United |
| 11 | Dave Hickson | February 14, 1953 | Manchester United |
| 12 | Duncan Ferguson | October 21, 1994 | Liverpool |

# ROYAL BLUE LEGENDS

While supporting the boys in royal blue has never been easy, to worship with Gwladys Street is a privilege... a pride... a passion of belonging to something unique. Long may it be so.

137

"*Merseyside folklore says that Liverpool play in red so that their blood will merge with the colour of their shirts - and that Everton wear royal blue for the same reason. Legend also has it that the Kop smiled every time that Alan Ball pulled on the red shirt of Arsenal.*"
Garry Doolan, *Liverpool Daily Post*

"*Without question, Alan Ball was the finest footballer that I had the good fortune to play alongside.*"
Howard Kendall

# ALAN BALL ...

Alan Ball was one of the greatest players ever to have played for Everton and England. I honestly believe that his immense contributions to England's World Cup triumph have never been fully recognised. Sir Alan Ball sounds about right! So for that matter does Sir Ray Wilson.

I hadn't seen much of Bally before the summer of 1966 but was aware that several top clubs were vying for his signature. In some small way I may have helped him pick Everton. Apparently when Harry Catterick was romancing him in 1965, Bally had watched us thrash Wednesday 5-1. I'd had a glory night and Bally was so impressed that he told the manager that he would join Everton only if he played alongside Alex Young. By the kick off of the 1966/67 season he had become Catterick's prized possession - a national hero captured from under Don Revie's nose.

Bally's impact on Merseyside was immediate. He tipped the scales in Everton's favour for several seasons after making a sensational Goodison debut against the Reds in which he grabbed two goals in the first 20 minutes. For the record he was the greatest footballer that I played with at Everton - an absolutely brilliant ball player who could create goals as well as score them. It was an honour to have played alongside him. In fact, Bally could do it all and would strut around the park with swaggering self-confidence. Surprisingly, he never looked that exceptional in practice but on matchdays the No 8 was perpetual motion for the full 90 minutes. He would run even harder when the chips were down.

We roomed together and I can definitely confirm that his enthusiasm was contagious. He was also a born motivator and simply hated to lose. If we had fallen behind at half-time, he would almost pull his hair out with frustration. And some times he would cry with anger in defeat. Bally demanded impeccably high standards and refused to accept anything less than 100%. Consequently, he was not shy to vent his frustrations and every so often would get himself into disciplinary trouble. But there again he wouldn't have been the player that he was without his combustible temperament. For someone who hated defeat, I was surprised that Bally loved horse-racing as much as he did. Of course he found no shortage of company among his team-mates for his racing excursions, but I was responsible for introducing him to the heartaches of being an owner. We bought a two-year old called 'Daxal'. Bally and Daxal - two thoroughbreds but only one of them was ever a winner.

Colin Harvey and Howard Kendall shared many of his qualities - tremendous appetites for work, immense courage and lots of skill. As a result, Everton constantly played through mid-field - much to the delight of the Goodison congregation. Sadly after capturing the championship, Catterick's young side was broken up. I believe that the demise started with Ball's transfer to Arsenal. The club reported that the sale made good business sense and claimed satisfaction with his five years of quality service and a 100% profit. To this day the Goodison faithful remain far less convinced.

Alex Young

"*Dixie Dean displayed tremendous courage and self-confidence, and maintained a positive attitude towards every game in which he competed. He was a magnificent ambassador for the club and was never cautioned or sent off in his career.*"
Sir Philip Carter, Everton chairman

"*It was an honour for me to play alongside Bill Dean. He loved the game and was respected by all. Every door on Merseyside was open to him.*"
Stan Bentham, player 1935/36-48/49 & coach

# DIXIE DEAN ...

Alan Shearer boards a bus in Newcastle city centre and indulges in banter with the fans en route to the match. He walks the last few yards to St James's Park through the crowds before knocking on the door to the players' entrance. A couple of hours later the England centre-forward plunges into action and bags a hat-trick to reach the amazing total of 60 League goals for the season. Fantasy? Yet rewind the time machine more than 70 years and substitute a tram for the bus, Goodison for St James's, Dean for Shearer and reality shimmers into focus.

William Ralph Dean - the greatest player of his generation and the finest centre-forward the game has known - was a touchable icon who used the tram to get to most home games. His record provides stark testimony to the transformation of our national game from a sport played by the people for the people to one in which today's public are unable to identify with footballers paid a king's ransom. Dean really did take a tram ride to immortality on May 5, 1928, when his three goals against Arsenal set what is surely one of those rare sporting records - an achievement cast in stone.

He was the original Roy of the Rovers with his fame crossing continents long before television had made football the global game it is today. Although I was never fortunate enough to see Dean play, my late father lauded his scoring talents and I did know the great man later in his life when I had the pleasure of interviewing him about his compelling career. I also had the poignant privilege of taking him as my Goodison guest to the game he died at, an ill-tempered Merseyside derby in March 1980.

If ever a player made a season his personal property, then 1927/28 belonged to Dean. George Camsell had struck 59 goals for Middlesbrough in Division 2 a year earlier and with two games left in 1928, the 21-year-old Everton scoring phenomenon was still seven goals away from overhauling that total. His four-goal blitz before half-time at Burnley set up an amazing climax to the campaign with Dean in search of a hat-trick in the final game at home to Arsenal. Although the Gunners took the lead after two minutes, Dean equalised within seconds with a thunderous shot from a Ted Critchley corner and then put Everton in front from the penalty spot after being brought down. The Londoners equalised and there were just eight minutes left when their goalkeeper turned over a George Martin shot to give Everton a corner at the Stanley Park end. The kick was delivered by Alec Troup and Dixie's head did the rest to complete his hat-trick. The crowd went ecstatic and a new entry was etched in the chronicles of our national game. The sustained celebrations included a pitch invasion with one brave fan planting a kiss on Dean's cheek before being removed by the constabulary. The impact of Dean's feat meant that Arsenal's late goal went virtually unnoticed and even Everton's championship presentation was overshadowed by his 60-goal record.

Dean's name was and still is synonymous with goals. I suspect that a century from now his goal-scoring achievements will still be recalled with an awesome respect bordering on incredulity.

John Keith

"*People forget that TG Jones was only 22 years of age when the war broke out. He had the world at his footballing feet. His thoughtful and skilful approach to defending was a revelation - decades ahead of his time. Goal-scorers have always hogged the headlines but TG was just as much a super-star as Bill Dean and Tom Lawton.*"
Gordon Watson

"*TG Jones simply oozed class.*"
Tommy Clinton, player 1948/49-53/54

# TG JONES ...

Thomas Gwynor Jones - better known to Evertonians as TG - was a truly exceptional talent. In the pre-war era when a defender's priorities were to make ferocious tackles and hoof the ball up field as far as possible, TG's exquisite footballing skills were a revelation. Goodison Park and the British game had never seen the likes of him before. He was a big lad and was dominant in the air, but it was his graceful abilities on the ground which made him so very, very special. TG always preferred to play his way out of trouble - with never a hint of a big hopeful clearance.

How good was he? It is no exaggeration to say that possibly he was the finest centre-half to have played the game! I remember reading that Bill Dean considered TG to be the best all-round player that he had ever played with or for that matter he had ever seen.

It is hard to believe that TG had featured in only half a dozen League games for Wrexham before moving to Goodison. In spite of his youth, his mental and physical maturity aided his rapid progress into a world-class defender. Initially the Everton fans would gasp as he weaved his way out of the penalty box, dribbling past one opponent after another before stroking inch-perfect passes to his forwards. But after only a handful of games both his team-mates and the fans on the terraces had fallen in love with his aristocratic play. He did everything with style. To see him take a free-kick was an education in itself. Invariably he would stroll up to the ball and effortlessly direct it 50 yards to a colleague with pin-point accuracy. He never failed.

TG was also a determined competitor and, along with the likes of Tommy Lawton and Joe Mercer, made a major contribution toward the successful League campaign in 1938/39. Lawton never relished the challenge of playing against his Everton team-mate on the international stage and believed that Jones was blessed with a golden right foot - the best in the business. Tragically TG managed to complete only two full seasons in the top flight before his career was interrupted by World War II. He was only 21 years of age when the 1939/40 League fixtures were cancelled. Nevertheless Jones demonstrated his commitment to Everton and, along with Theo Kelly, worked hard at keeping the club going in regional football. Although TG served in the RAF, he managed to turn out for the Blues whenever he could. In fact he played in 23 war-time Merseyside derbies, even at centre-forward on one occasion, and was reported to have played some of the best football of his career in war-time competitions for Everton and Wales.

It is sad that after the cessation of hostilities TG played fewer than 100 post-war games before turning his back on first-class football in 1950. After a series of disagreements with new Everton boss Cliff Britton, he opted to run the Tower Hotel in Pwllheli and join the local club in the Welsh League. His departure coincided with a major decline in Everton's fortunes and the subsequent relegation to Division 2.

Even though World War II had sabotaged his playing career, I recall that TG Jones enhanced every game in which he played. I feel privileged to have seen him play.

*Jim King*

Jim King

"*Howard Kendall was an exceptionally talented player respected as a tremendous tackler and a perceptive passer of the ball. He shared many of the qualities of Colin Harvey and Alan Ball. All three had powerful engines, genuine appetites for work, immense courage and lots and lots of skill.*"
Alex Young

"*Howard Kendall is the only individual qualified to be enshrined in the Hall of Fame as a player and as a manager. In both capacities, he transformed the club's expectations and beliefs into glittering prizes. Kendall should be remembered for the great success he brought to Everton.*"
Professor Tom Cannon, Everton Shareholders' Association

# HOWARD KENDALL ...

Howard Kendall was heralded as the final piece of Harry Catterick's jigsaw - a big-money acquisition with the added label of being the youngest player to feature in an FA Cup final. I liked Howard from the start. He was my kind of player - someone who combined style with honest endeavour. Although famed for his fierce tackling, there was more to his game than mere strength and courage. He was also an astute reader of the game and a tremendous first-time passer of the ball.

Away from the thunder of the football battlefield, Howard always displayed a decent sense of humour. I remember that he had not been at Everton very long when we had to make the long trek to Portman Road. On the return journey we would take a coach from Ipswich to London and then hop on a train to Lime Street. It was a long trip and we never got back before midnight. Howard had arranged to see a friend somewhere in Derbyshire and was to catch a different train out of Euston. But before our departures, he had made the mistake of telling some of the lads that he had a few bottles of wine in his bag for the weekend. Just before our train departed we distracted him and replaced his refreshments with ballast made up of old shorts and socks. Well you should have seen his face as our train pulled away from the platform with West, Royle and Morrissey toasting him with his own wines. For the record I think that his taste that day was something like *Mateus Rose* or some other red rubbish.

Of course, I can't pay tribute to 'Kendall - The Player' without mentioning his famous side-kicks. The mid-field unit of Kendall, Harvey & Ball developed a kind of telepathic understanding and played beautiful football. Gordon West would joke that Kendall, Harvey & Ball were the only three-man team to have won the League championship! Of course, Howard was an ace in his own right - a footballer of genuine international quality. I recall that after the championship side had been dismantled, he almost single-handedly kept the club away from the relegation trap-door.

Several years later Howard returned to revitalise the fortunes of the club. His record confirms that he was no ordinary manager and under his guidance Everton captured two Division 1 titles, a European trophy and also appeared in five Wembley finals. The success of 'Kendall - The Manager' was founded on his keen eye for talent and his knack for getting the best out of his players. Despite having to operate on a shoe-string, he was able to attract the likes of Southall, Reid, Gray, Sheedy and Mountfield as well as Beardsley and Hutchison. Obviously he should never have left for Bilbao and should never have returned to the Goodison hot-seat for a second stint never mind a third.

He brought glittering rewards to Goodison as a player and as a manager. But perhaps more than anything I think of 'Kendall - The Evertonian' - someone who never disguised his genuine love for Everton. A commitment demonstrated by the fact that he travelled all the way from sunny Greece to attend the Hall of Fame Dinner in March 1999. The emotional reception which he received that night confirmed his very special place in the hearts of fellow Evertonians, both young and old.

Brian Labone

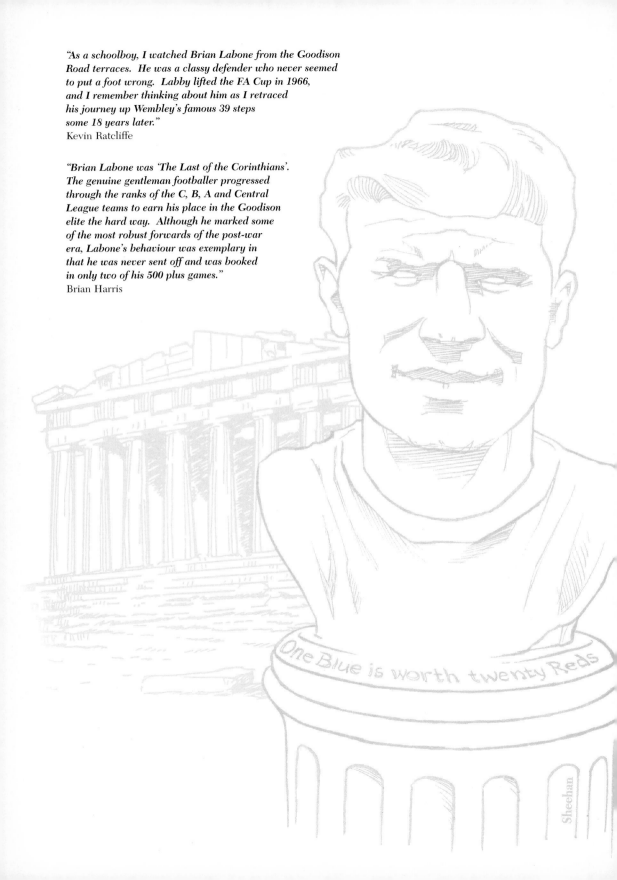

"As a schoolboy, I watched Brian Labone from the Goodison Road terraces. He was a classy defender who never seemed to put a foot wrong. Labby lifted the FA Cup in 1966, and I remember thinking about him as I retraced his journey up Wembley's famous 39 steps some 18 years later."
Kevin Ratcliffe

"Brian Labone was 'The Last of the Corinthians'. The genuine gentleman footballer progressed through the ranks of the C, B, A and Central League teams to earn his place in the Goodison elite the hard way. Although he marked some of the most robust forwards of the post-war era, Labone's behaviour was exemplary in that he was never sent off and was booked in only two of his 500 plus games."
Brian Harris

One Blue is worth twenty Reds

# BRIAN LABONE ...

For someone who was learning to toddle when 'The Last of the Corinthians' had already mastered the art of climbing up the steps to the royal box at Wembley and grasping the old silver cup, it is difficult for me to comment on a footballing legend who played 26 times for England and nearly 20 times that number for Everton. But I have no hesitation in confirming that Brian Labone is one of us. He feels the same highs and lows as the rest of us, week in - week out.

Labone seems to have been on the Goodison scene all of my life. I have been told that I was only seven months old when I caught my first glimpse of him. Apparently, I was perched on my dad's shoulders somewhere along Queen's Drive when the proud royal blue skipper waved the FA Cup in my direction. But my first real memory of the Everton icon came a few years later when my dad won a few quid on Labone's aptly named horse 'Goodison' as part of an ITV Seven. Now that was a victory celebration. By the time I was privileged to be taken to Goodison Park to see the Blues, the 1969/70 championship team had been broken up and Labone's career had been cruelly finished by injury. I remember that his withdrawal from the 1971 semi-final turned the game in Liverpool's favour and, of course, my dad's unwavering assertion that the big No 5 embodied everything that was special about Everton - skill, strength, style and dignity. Over the next couple of years my dad would occasionally point out the tall, increasingly portly figure of Labone on Goodison Road on matchdays. My dad would always make the same comment: "*You would have loved him son, you would have loved him.*"

Sometimes Labone would be featured in the local media, usually before cup finals and Merseyside derbies. He always came across as a gentleman and a genuine Evertonian, someone who, whatever he had achieved in a royal blue shirt and whatever he was doing in his life, was first and foremost a blue-blood. In the early 1990s, as one of the people involved in *When Skies Are Grey*, I had the honour to interview him for our 'Talking Blues' series. Of course I was aware that meeting someone you had admired all of your life could be a let down. I feared that actually talking to the same 'Last of the Corinthians' that my dad had worshiped would be nerve-wracking. But Brian Labone was simply great - everything that I had wanted him to be. First and foremost his love of Everton was clearly evident. And perhaps more than anything, his genuine humility shone through. He couldn't understand why three lads who had never seen him play wanted to listen to him. I must add that he was also very funny - in a middle-aged sort of way.

Over the past few years Labone has returned to the Goodison fold and can be seen on the pitch chaperoning the match-ball sponsors before the kick off and presenting the 'Golden Goal' prizes at half-time. These activities wouldn't appeal to many ex-stars but Labone has always wanted to be close to the public who had paid his wages for so many years. When modern stars have faded away, I have no doubts that Brian Labone will remain a much loved, greatly respected blue-blood.

Phil Redmond

"*Bob Latchford was as good a goal-scorer as any in the post-war era and like Graeme Sharp, a decade later, was grossly under-rated. Latch hit his peak during the 1977/78 season. In the early part of that season his physical presence and appetite for goals simply overwhelmed defences, especially away from home. Two away games stand out in my memory. I recall that he scored four in our 5-1 victory at QPR and grabbed another in a similar 5-1 demolition at Leicester. Latch could have doubled his account at Filbert Street but after side-stepping goalkeeper Mark Wallington, he and the ball drifted into my path. Of course, I pushed him out of the way and tucked the ball into the net. Latch was far from pleased and literally chased me back to the half-way line. Goals were important to Bob Latchford. Goals were his life-blood.*"*
Duncan McKenzie, player 1976/77-77/78

*Latchford was my hero. Big Bob was always in the right place at the right time. I used to watch him when I was a schoolboy and try to copy him. He was excellent at arriving at the near post before defenders and getting that important touch.*"*
Ian Rush, boyhood Everton fan

# BOB LATCHFORD ...

Big Bob was the right man in the right place at the wrong time. He was one of the finest marksmen of his generation - a bustling No 9 in the true Everton tradition. But he had the misfortune to parade his talents at a time when the only silverware to land on Merseyside went to the other side of Stanley Park. However, Big Bob's consolation was that he was the man who enabled Evertonians to hold their heads up high.

Latchford was a swashbuckling striker who specialised in thrilling diving headers and at the conclusion of the 1977/78 season proved himself to be the best in the country. That was when he became the first player in six seasons to net 30 League goals - and win a £10,000 prize from a national newspaper. It also led to a short-lived interest from myself in the delights of horticulture. Carried away by the emotion of the occasion that April afternoon, I am embarrassed to admit that I clambered over the safety railings at the Gwladys Street end and raced onto the turf. One lightning fast fan had already snatched up the entire penalty spot so I had to make do with a portion of pitch from where I imagined Latchford had headed his twenty-ninth goal. That emerald green turf grew in a plastic ice-cream container by the side of my bed - until my father forced me to transplant it and fill the bald spot under my sister's swing. My family has long since moved but whoever lives at 6 Byland Close in Formby may be interested to learn that a piece of Goodison history still grows beyond their kitchen window.

Symbolically, Latchford scored his thirtieth goal almost 50 years on from the day of the original individual goal-scoring achievement - Dean's sixtieth League goal. Like Dixie, Big Bob was a hero, a legend, an awe inspiring figure. And what's more, he is a thoroughly decent bloke, too.

I first met my hero, that is if you don't count a very brief flirtation on the pitch at Hillsborough after the 1977 League Cup final replay when I peered through the snorkel of my parka, squeaked *"Great goal, Bob"* and patted his broad, sweaty back before being chased off by a steward, at a celebration of Everton centre-forwards in the early 1990s. Gary Lineker, Andy Gray, Graeme Sharp, Alex Young and Dave Hickson were all present but I only wanted an audience with one man. I caught up with him after the dinner, when he was trying to make sense of a clearly worse-for-wear former-colleague. I introduced myself as a fan of his, rather than a reporter and offered to buy him a drink. *"No, that's all right"* Big Bob said firmly. *"I'll buy you one!"*

Twenty minutes later, after sharing countless tales of Latchford goals (there were 138 to choose from and the only one he couldn't remember was the 1977 diving header off the floor into the roof of the Gwladys Street net against Manchester City) I noticed that I was surrounded by the friends I had travelled to the dinner with. Wide-eyed and reverent, they were all muttering variations of the same sentence: *"Hush! Dave's talking to Big Bob!"*

To thirty-somethings weaned on a diet of Goodison woe, Big Bob had that heroic aura. He scored goals. He wore the No 9 shirt. And he stands his round!

*Dad Prentice*

David Prentice

"*Tommy Lawton was my schoolboy hero. I saw most of his pre-war appearances from the boys' pen. Admission in those days cost 4d but was worth every brass farthing. Lawton had every attribute that a centre-forward should have - he was two-footed, dominant in the air and ran opponents ragged with his pace and intelligent positional play. In my opinion, he was on a par with Dixie Dean. Regrettably Lawton's career at Everton was too short - but long remembered. It was a sad day when he left for London and the championship team effectively broke up.*"
Norman Dainty, Everton Shareholders' Association

"*Although I was too young to have seen him play, I was raised on stories of Tommy Lawton. He was my idea of the complete centre-forward - immaculate on the ground and a true star in the air.*"
Fred Pickering, player 1963/64-66/67

# TOMMY LAWTON ...

As an Everton No 9, Tommy Lawton could do it all. And that's no exaggeration. He was strong and could hold the ball up, he was athletic and could dribble at speed, he packed a powerful shot in both feet and also was a terrific header of the ball. And in the eyes of mere mortals, he exhibited all of these abilities but at the same time always looked immaculate with never a hair out of place.

I had played against him during his early days at Burnley and was impressed. Lawton swiftly earned a reputation for being a very gifted goal-scorer and arrived at Goodison not long afterwards as a replacement for Bill Dean. For a boy of 17, he didn't seem to be fazed by the challenge of replacing a blue-blooded legend. Of course, comparisons with Dean are inevitable. But from my privileged position of having played with both of them, I disagree with those who argue that Dean was the more prolific striker and Lawton was the better player. Lawton was a world-class player but, in my opinion, no one was better than Bill Dean - not even Tommy Lawton.

Of course it goes without saying that Dean was the greatest header of the ball that the game has ever known. Nevertheless Lawton wasn't too far behind thanks to Dean, who worked hard in training at helping his prodigy enhance his aerial skills. In the absence of a team manager, it was common for the Everton players to assist one another. For example Joe Mercer and I would toil for hours at improving our passing game. And as half-backs, we also practiced throw-ins by hurling a type of medicine ball against the old Park End stand. We took turns at throwing the medicine ball above a blue line drawn about 10 feet from the ground. Dean and Lawton adopted a similar approach at honing their heading skills. The rest us would marvel as they played head-tennis with the medicine ball. We were amazed they could head the same heavy ball which Joe and I had difficulty throwing. As a direct consequence of Dean's tutoring, Lawton became expert at heading a regular football with accuracy and power.

Tommy Lawton was a key member of a very young Everton team which included Joe Mercer, TG Jones, Torry Gillick, Alex Stevenson and Ted Sagar. Labelled 'The School of Science', we were not encumbered by elaborate tactics. We were free to improvise and prided ourselves on playing fast, flowing football. Lawton scored 34 times in 38 League outings during the 1938/39 championship season and we were poised to dominate English football for another decade or so. Of course, we were all devastated by the outbreak of World War II just three League games into the new campaign. Shortly afterwards, Lawton joined the Army and I must confess that he was never quite the same. The war made him more worldly and far less content with life on Merseyside.

Even though his demeanour had an unsettling impact on the team, it was a very sad day when he moved down south. Lawton had been expected to fill the Goodison trophy cabinet with silverware, but Evertonians shouldn't feel cheated that he played less than 100 games. With Bill Dean approaching the twilight of his career, Everton were very fortunate to have unearthed another world-class spearhead. And without question, Tommy Lawton was world-class!

Gordon Watson

*"Reidy was a combative mid-fielder who pulled no punches. He always gave his best for Everton and it is hardly surprising that the club has never been able to replace him."*
Shea Neary, WBU light-weight champion

*"The Everton side in the mid-1980s was the greatest of all and Peter Reid epitomised that era more than anyone. Had it not been for the Heysel tragedy, Reid and Everton would have gone on to conquer Europe and the world."*
Derek Hatton, *Talk Radio*

# PETER REID ...

Peter Reid was a member of the most successful Everton side ever, a team who played beautiful football, but without his mid-field mastery it is doubtful whether either would have been so. It is often said that royal blue fortunes were revived the moment Kevin Brock's weak back-pass failed to get to the Oxford goalkeeper and Adrian Heath nipped in to equalise for the Blues in a League Cup tie back in January 1984.
But I beg to differ.

For me, the new beginning happened four months earlier at Tottenham, when Peter Reid, making his first appearance in the royal blue No 6 shirt he was to make his own, slid in for the first goal in a 2-1 victory. The fixture had produced no Everton win during the previous decade and the result confirmed that Howard Kendall had got the footings in place. The team were playing to feet. And with the imminent arrival of Andy Gray, the Englishman from Huyton and the Scot from Glasgow were to boss the revival. The irony is that Reid could have become an Evertonian in the summer of 1980 when Gordon Lee agreed a £600,000 fee with Bolton Wanderers but his personal terms could not be met. Arsenal were also interested and Wolves in fact agreed to his terms but offered only £450,000. As a consequence Reid stayed at Bolton awaiting the expiration of his contract but his bad luck with injuries continued and Wolves went to the wall both on and off the pitch. Following an earlier broken kneecap and then a right knee damaged when he went down in a heap with George Wood and which was to keep him out for over a year, he then endured a cartilage operation and a broken leg after that. I recall that Reid was even on the point of signing for Sheffield Wednesday when Howard Kendall came in with a knock-down £60,000 offer in December 1982.

Reid managed to play only seven League games during the remainder of the 1982/83 season, all in the unfamiliar No 10 shirt wide on the right, the first of them in a 3-1 win against Forest alongside the treacherous Steve McMahon. After that important result at White Hart Lane he played three more games, scoring twice, and then was dropped. Characteristically he fought his way back into the side - as a late sub in the League Cup fixture against Coventry with the Blues down 0-1 in front of 9,080 hardy souls. Reid changed the outcome of that game with a couple of penetrating runs and helped inspire a 2-1 win with Graeme Sharp obliging in the last minute. As a result, he not surprisingly became a permanent fixture in the Everton side. His instinctive, incisive passes and vigorous but fair tackles were a feature of the team's play in two championship seasons - his dark brown hair turning more and more grey each game.

Even though Reidy was not captain, his influence on all those around him was immense. He was a battler who led by example and his never-say-die enthusiasm meant that Everton were rarely beaten - and never until the very end. Reid was the axis of a great side and was instrumental in the club reaching four Wembley finals in 26 months. My abiding memory of the 1986 FA Cup final, his exquisite pass to release Lineker past Hand-sen for the opening goal apart, was his appearance at the pre-match pitch inspection with his hair dyed Ronald Reagan-black especially for the occasion and resplendent in a baggy suit. Without doubt, Peter Reid was a one-off!

Mark Tallentire

"Graeme Sharp was one of the best leaders of the line in the modern game and was the focal point for much of Everton's play during the most rewarding period in the club's history. He was a striker who displayed Scottish commitment and passion but also possessed skill and poise. A scorer of both simple and extra-ordinary goals, Sharp was a marksman of genuine quality and a truly gifted footballer."
Mike Hughes, *BBC Radio Merseyside*

"Everton have had some great No 9s. Names like Dean, Lawton, Young, Latchford, Gray and Sharp come to mind. Graeme Sharp always wore the famous blue and white of Everton with real pride. He ranks second only to Dixie Dean on the list of Everton goal-scorers."
Dave Hickson

# GRAEME SHARP ...

Whenever the playing career of Graeme Sharp is reviewed, he is too often described simply as 'a scorer of spectacular goals'. Of course Sharp contributed some truly amazing strikes but I recall that there was so much more to his game. In my opinion he was, without question, the most complete British centre-forward of his generation. I must confess that he was my boyhood favourite - an icon to all young impressionable Evertonians throughout the eighties when the most successful team in the club's history was blessed with many heroes.

In the illustrious history of Everton, I think that Graeme Sharp has had few equals. He was a fine footballer and a consistent performer as well as a fierce competitor, capable of rousing souls and filling bellies with Scottish fire, and led the Everton attack with a combination of power, grace and menace. The big centre-forward possessed many skills and even refined backing into a defender to earn a free kick into an art form. In the air, he was breath-taking. Every header was timed to perfection and executed with style. He seemed to hang longer in the air so that we could all appreciate the moment. On the floor his control and vision were equally refined and it became standard practice for strikers of the calibre of Adrian Heath, Andy Gray, Gary Lineker and Tony Cottee to proclaim that Sharp was the best partner that they had ever had - and for Ian Rush to confide that Sharp was the best that he had not.

Unfortunately Sharp's true worth was never fully appreciated beyond the boundaries of Merseyside, except for maybe by Scotland boss Jock Stein. Although international recognition seemed to be consolation enough at the time, it still irritates me that the magnificence of the Everton spearhead was not universally acknowledged. As usual, it was left to Evertonians to enjoy Sharp's true class and his immense contributions to the club's period of dominance in the 1980s. He was a very special player - respected by football fans of all ages. The only gripe that I have ever heard murmured about his performances was that his goal return did not match his lauded creative talents. I think that such criticism is a little harsh because he amassed 158 goals during his days at Everton. In fact the record books show that Sharp is Everton's top post-war marksman, the club's second leading goal-scorer of all time - second only to Dixie Dean, and a striker whose goal collection is over-brimming with, well, the spectacular!

Even though I have stressed that Sharp was much more than a scorer of spectacular goals, I cannot overlook the fact that he did bag more than his share of exquisitely executed headers and shots. The best? Who hasn't, in a moment of intoxicated or euphoric clarity, transported themselves back to Anfield and wallowed in the immortal words of Match of the Day's John Motson on October 20, 1984: *"Reid to Stevens looking for Sharp... he's got behind Lawrenson... Sharp!!! What a fantastic goal! An unbelievable finish from Graeme Sharp! I haven't seen a goal quite like that in a Merseyside derby for years. And the Evertonians have gone berserk! Absolutely marvellous to see him get behind the defender and take it first time on the volley giving Grobbelaar no chance."*

Andy Hunter

"Neville Southall is the best goalkeeper that I have seen at Goodison over the past 50 years and possibly the best of all time. I believe that the key to his success was his tremendous powers of concentration. During his heyday, his Everton team-mates would dominate most opponents and Southall would not be required to participate in perhaps 75 minutes of the game. But when called on to pull off an important save or two, he did so with much confidence and little fanfare. Although not the most commanding of goalkeepers in dealing with crosses and wrapped up in cotton wool like all modern keepers, Southall was nevertheless a world-class No 1."
Jimmy O'Neill, player 1950/51-59/60

"Neville Southall was my best signing in terms of years service and turned out to be, in my opinion, the best goalkeeper in the world."
Howard Kendall

# NEVILLE SOUTHALL ...

As a kid I was brain-washed by tales of the exploits of Ted Sagar and other Everton legends. But I suppose that it wasn't until we signed Gordon West from Blackpool in 1962 that I realised that a goalie can be every ounce a match-winner as a star forward. West was a tremendous goalkeeper with great hands and cat-like reflexes and, as a result, a decade of Everton custodians found him to be a very hard act to follow. That is until Neville Southall showed up with a curriculum vitae punctuated with spells at Bury, Winsford United and, of course, Llandudno Council. Despite his modest pedigree, or perhaps inspired by it, Big Nev quickly developed into a world-class goalie as well as a world-class character.

It would be easy to wax lyrical about the big man's shot-stopping abilities and reel off his long list of match-winning saves. But my fondest memories are of his pre-match antics. All Evertonians know that Goodison was never the most brilliant place at 2.30 p.m. on a Saturday - you sheltered from the polluted wind which whistled across Stanley Park, your pie was Chernobyl hot and the DJ played songs that made you cringe. However, your mood warmed up when the big man rolled onto the pitch to receive a terrific reception from the Gwladys Street end.

As the first practice shot flew towards his goal, Big Nev would launch himself into space. The ball was palmed away and within one nano-second the big man was back on his feet, as if the grass was a green trampoline. Another shot smashed towards him and this time his massive hands plucked it out of the air as if it was a satsuma. The breath-taking display continued for twenty minutes while his less hardy team-mates drifted towards the comfort of the tunnel. Not Big Nev, he would stand quietly defiant muddied from head-to-toe with his socks around his ankles and looked as if he had just completed the Grand National without a horse. In fact if you had had a few beers, one look at Nev would make you think that your Timex had stopped in the Winslow and that you had missed the match. But his camouflage simply reflected his commitment to perfection and to the high standards which he demanded of himself and his colleagues.

When squad numbers were introduced by the Premier League, there was no doubt about who would wear Everton's No 1. It wasn't just because Big Nev was the established goalkeeper, it was a tribute to the fact that during the mid-1980s he had been the best in the world. Although the Heysel tragedy denied him a European stage, Neville Southall was hailed along side the giants of the past like Lev Yashin and Gordon Banks.

To the Goodison fans, he was like a big brother who would chase all the bullies away. When we felt threatened someone would say: "*Don't worry Nev will save it!*" and more times than not he did. He will always be one of Goodison's favourite sons - you could say that he remains the 'Keeper of the Faith'. I can't imagine that there will ever be another like him. I think that the club should honour Neville Southall by retiring his No 1 shirt number.

George Orr

"Waggy is everything that a central defender should be.  As veteran of over 500 games in the top flight with Everton, his speed of thought has not diminished and still enables him to master the pace of the younger generation of opponents.  As a skipper, he has always marshalled his troops with intelligent commitment and successfully navigated the club through some troubled waters in recent years."
Brian Labone

"Although Waggy is an ex-Red from the backwaters of Norfolk, he has never let Everton down.  In fact, every Evertonian is indebted to him.  But for his inspirational leadership both on and off the pitch after Joe Royle quit, Everton would have been relegated.  Caretaker Watson came to the rescue and steadied the ship in 1997 and has excelled at instilling calmness and steel at the heart of the defence during the relegation battles of the past few seasons.  His true value is evident when his name is missing from the team-sheet."
Ian MacDonald, Independent Blues

# DAVE WATSON ...

What can you write about Dave Watson that hasn't already been said? Well the first time I laid eyes on him I can honestly say that I hated him. The reason being that his predecessor was one of my favourite players. Derek Mountfield, a true blue Evertonian, was brave, comfortable on the ball and possessed the uncanny knack of popping up at the other end of the pitch to score vital goals. Way back in 1986, I could not understand why Everton had bought an Anfield reject from Norwich to replace him. To be quite honest I thought that we had wasted £900,000. How wrong I was!

Today, how could anyone dislike Dave Watson? The Everton No 5 epitomises everything that is good about football. Even though his first season (one in which Everton romped away with the League title) got off to something of a shaky start, since then Watson has been the model of consistency. His mistakes at Goodison can be counted on the fingers of one hand. His commitment is unquestionable, his bravery undoubted, his loyalty unrivalled. And with so many players worshipping the god of money, Dave Watson is one of a dying breed - a footballer whose primary motivation is to play football and to play for Everton. He is a man, like me and you, who would have paid money to pull on the famous royal blue shirt and run out at Goodison. I doubt if we will ever see his like again - someone playing 500 games for Everton at the highest level and enjoying every minute.

Watson's international career never really got off the ground but England's loss was definitely Everton's gain. His meagre tally of 12 full caps was mainly due to England's embarrassment of talent at centre-back during the late eighties coupled with the fact that he played for a less fashionable northern club. Also with only two major honours at either end of his career (the League championship in 1986/87 and the FA Cup in 1995) Watson has been unlucky to have played mainly in struggling Everton sides. But who will ever forget the expression on his face as he lifted the FA Cup? He looked like he was going to burst with pride. Here was a man who shared the joy of the other Evertonians on Wembley's terraces - you had no doubt about that. And you never had any doubts about his commitment toward the royal blue cause.

Dave Watson was never a fancy player. He wouldn't embark on jinking runs or attempt to spray passes 50 yards across the park - that wasn't his game. Perhaps his greatest quality was that he knew his own strengths and weaknesses. As a result he was virtually peerless in the things that he did well - the simple things like heading, tackling, marking, reading the game and marshalling those around him.

As a thirty something myself I feel like I have grown up with the Everton No 5. For fans like me it will be a very sad day when he finally hangs up his boots. But with youngsters like Richard Gough at his side, I wouldn't write Dave Watson off just yet - people have been making that mistake for the past five years.

Mark Staniford

"'I don't know if many churches have a football pitch in their backyard but I suspect that no other has had 'The Golden Vision' as a neighbour. During the 1960s - even at the height of Beatlemania - Alex Young was exalted in a manner experienced by very few mortals on Merseyside."*
Reverend Harry Ross, St Luke the Evangelist

*"Those who did not see him play will never entirely understand why those of us who did remain convinced that Young was better than Pele, Best, Eusabio and anyone else who graced Goodison during the sixties. Alex Young was elegance personified. His ball control was infallible and he never failed to tame the ball no matter how hard, high or fast it came to him. But perhaps his greatest asset - his very uniqueness - lay in the way he looked playing the game. Young did everything with style and, when at his best, he transported Evertonians to royal blue heaven. Whether or not his moves came off, he never compromised the beautiful game and never resorted to the banal, dull or dirty. No player, before or since, has come close to achieving the sheer beauty of his play."*
Phil Pellow, *Satis?*

# ALEX YOUNG ...

When I think of the beautiful game, instinctively I think of Alex Young - the most stylish British footballer of his day. Since his Everton debut in late-1960, generations of Evertonians have worshiped him. For fans under 40 who may not have seen him play, I can confirm the tales that Young simply ghosted past defenders and left them rooted to the spot with a combination of intricate footwork, delicate feints and elegant body swerves. He was elegant but never ostentatious.

Some years later, the BBC broadcast my film 'The Golden Vision' which sought to capture the adulation of Everton fans for their idol - Alex Young. The film's title resulted from a chat with Danny Blanchflower. The former-Spurs star claimed that the essence of life for the most passionate fans, many of whom are poor and led lives of drudgery, was the 90 minutes at the end of the week when they lived out their dream - it was their golden vision. On the blue side of the Mersey, Alex Young personified that vision. He was a blonde genius - gifted enough to be grouped with the likes of Pele, Cruyff and Best. Everyone at Goodison worshiped him, that is everyone except Harry Catterick. The Everton manager had tried to replace Young with Fred Pickering, a big-money buy from Blackburn, and Joe Royle, a 16-year-old prodigy. But the Goodison faithful would have none of it and continued to demand the silky skills of their idol.

I think it's only fair to say that during the making of the film our interactions with Catterick were far from cordial. For some reason the club was suspicious of our motives and even charged us £75 every time we took the cameras into Goodison. By comparison, Alex was a gentleman as well as a consummate professional. At the beginning of the film, director Ken Loach and the crew set up at the Gwladys Street end to record a dream sequence in which Ken Jones, who played Uncle Sid, was supposed to execute a diving header into the net. There was Ken and Alex attired in royal blue and five Everton apprentices, including a young Roger Kenyon, masquerading as the opposition. Alex centred, Ken missed. Alex centred, Ken stumbled. Alex centred, Ken connected but the ball went wide. Alex got it right every single time but Ken was like an Everton jigsaw of a more recent era. Suddenly there was a scream from an irate figure in the tunnel: *"What the effing hell do you think you are doing on the pitch! Don't you know it's not for playing on!"* We had permission to be there and had paid our £75 but nobody had told the groundsman.

Alex even provided us with the perfect ending. We filmed the visit of Sheffield United and with one minute to go he collected the ball on the right, cut inside the box, beat one defender, waltzed around another and accelerated past a third. Alex paused near the penalty spot, psyched-out Alan Hodgkinson, the Blades' keeper, and calmly placed the ball into the middle of the net - precisely where our cameraman Tony Imi was focusing. Unfortunately Tony had just run out of film!

Alex Young was our golden vision - we worshiped him. I often think of those wonderful days in the sixties watching him float across the Goodison pitch. Thirty years on, the vision has not faded.

Neville Smith

Neville Smith

The Hall of Fame concept was designed to embrace inputs from players, shareholders and season-ticket holders. Hundreds of fans have provided details of their top 10s - their all-time Toffee favourites ...

### ARTHUR ABERCROMBY

1  Roy Vernon
2  Neville Southall
3  Alan Ball
4  Peter Reid
5  Joe Royle
6  Dave Hickson
7  Howard Kendall
8  Colin Harvey
9  Bobby Collins
10 Alex Parker

*Everton director*

### RAY HALL

1  Alan Ball
2  Colin Harvey
3  Neville Southall
4  Howard Kendall
5  Brian Labone
6  Ray Wilson
7  Bob Latchford
8  Colin Todd
9  Gary Lineker
10 Tommy Wright

*youth academy director*

### ALEX SCOTT

1  Alex Young
2  Ray Wilson
3  Dixie Dean
4  Brian Labone
5  Bobby Collins
6  Joe Mercer
7  Alan Ball
8  Trevor Steven
9  Sandy Brown
10 Gary Stevens

*former-player*

### DEREK HATTON

1  Peter Reid
2  Trevor Steven
3  Alan Ball
4  Alex Young
5  Dave Hickson
6  Tony Kay
7  Howard Kendall
8  Kevin Ratcliffe
9  Neville Southall
10 Duncan McKenzie

*Talk Radio*

### KEVIN CAMPBELL

1  Dixie Dean
2  TG Jones
3  Joe Mercer
4  Alan Ball
5  Colin Harvey
6  Howard Kendall
7  Cliff Britton
8  Neville Southall
9  Dave Watson
10 Dave Hickson

*Everton player*

### TONY LLOYD

1  Duncan McKenzie
2  Andy Gray
3  Peter Reid
4  Brian Labone
5  Alex Young
6  Dave Hickson
7  Dave Watson
8  Joe Royle
9  Alan Ball
10 Dixie Dean

*Investors In Everton*

### TG JONES

1  Ted Sagar
2  Tommy Lawton
3  Dixie Dean
4  Joe Mercer
5  Stan Bentham
6  Gordon Watson
7  Jackie Coulter
8  Warney Cresswell
9  Alex Stevenson
10 Torry Gillick

*former-player*

### TONY McNAMARA

1  Tommy Lawton
2  Alex Young
3  TG Jones
4  Tommy Eglington
5  Alan Ball
6  Trevor Steven
7  Brian Labone
8  Dave Thomas
9  Bobby Collins
10 Ted Sagar

*former-player*

### ED STEWART

1  Bob Latchford
2  Neville Southall
3  Dave Watson
4  Kevin Ratcliffe
5  Peter Reid
6  Kevin Sheedy
7  Andrei Kanchelskis
8  Peter Farrell
9  Dave Thomas
10 Gordon Watson

*BBC Radio 2*

### ANDY McCORMICK

1  Joe Mercer
2  Peter Reid
3  Dave Hickson
4  Brian Labone
5  Kevin Sheedy
6  Alex Young
7  Tony Kay
8  Paul Bracewell
9  Ray Wilson
10 Alan Ball

*Everton fan*
*Liverpool*

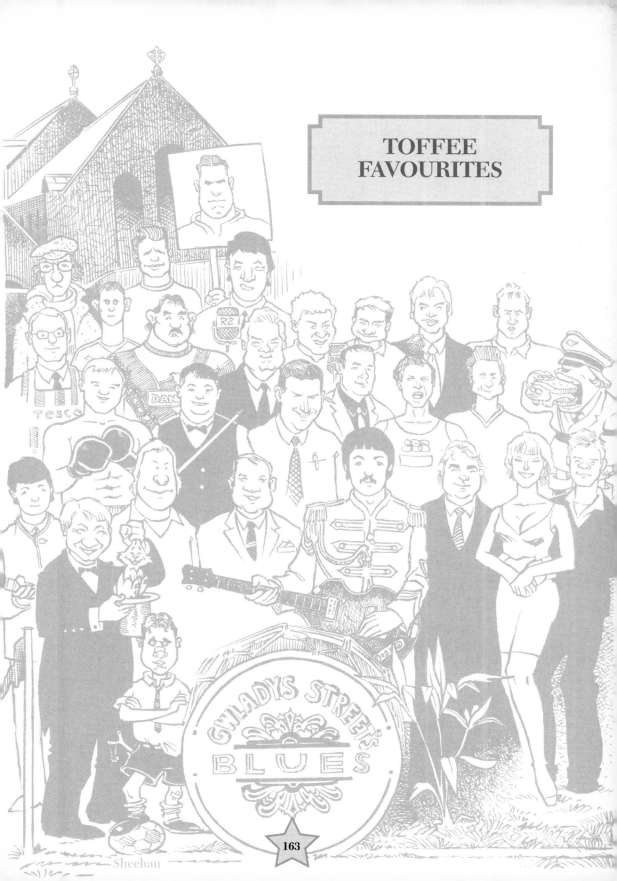

TOFFEE
FAVOURITES

GWLADYS STREET'S BLUES

Sheehan

163

The blue side of the Mersey have fielded some of the most gifted
footballers in the history of the English game ...

### LORD GRANTCHESTER

1 Alan Ball
2 Alex Young
3 Roy Vernon
4 Trevor Steven
5 Peter Reid
6 Brian Labone
7 Kevin Ratcliffe
8 Neville Southall
9 Colin Harvey
10 Gary Lineker

*Everton director*

### PHIL JEAVONS

1 Nick Barmby
2 Dave Watson
3 Peter Reid
4 Neville Southall
5 Duncan Ferguson
6 Andrei Kanchelskis
7 Joe Royle
8 Dixie Dean
9 Joe Parkinson
10 Andy Hinchcliffe

*Everton player*

### PAUL BRACEWELL

1 Neville Southall
2 Dave Watson
3 Peter Reid
4 Andy Gray
5 Gary Lineker
6 Adrian Heath
7 Kevin Ratcliffe
8 Trevor Steven
9 Graeme Sharp
10 Kevin Sheedy

*former-player*

### JOHN PARROTT

1 Neville Southall
2 Graeme Sharp
3 Gary Lineker
4 Dave Watson
5 Andy Gray
6 Peter Reid
7 Paul Bracewell
8 Trevor Steven
9 Kevin Ratcliffe
10 Kevin Sheedy

*former-snooker
world champion*

### STUART BARLOW

1 Neville Southall
2 Peter Beardsley
3 Dave Watson
4 Peter Reid
5 Dixie Dean
6 Bob Latchford
7 Jimmy Gabriel
8 Colin Harvey
9 Trevor Steven
10 Kevin Ratcliffe

*former-player*

### ROGER LONG

1 Dixie Dean
2 Alex Young
3 Neville Southall
4 Ted Sagar
5 Howard Kendall
6 Colin Harvey
7 Graeme Sharp
8 Roy Vernon
9 Kevin Ratcliffe
10 Bob Latchford

*Everton fan
Richmond*

### KEN REA

1 Dixie Dean
2 TG Jones
3 Tommy Lawton
4 Tommy Eglington
5 Brian Labone
6 Tommy Jones
7 Alex Parker
8 Peter Farrell
9 Bobby Collins
10 Colin Harvey

*former-player*

### LEN CAPELING

1 Alan Ball
2 Alex Young
3 Roy Vernon
4 Ray Wilson
5 Peter Reid
6 Brian Labone
7 Howard Kendall
8 Colin Harvey
9 Andy Gray
10 Gary Lineker

*Liverpool Daily Post*

### SUSAN PALMER

1 Dixie Dean
2 Howard Kendall
3 Alan Ball
4 Colin Harvey
5 Neville Southall
6 Dave Watson
7 Dave Hickson
8 Brian Labone
9 Joe Mercer
10 Duncan Ferguson

*Bellefield administration*

*"Everton has been noted for the high quality of its football. It has been an unwritten but rigid policy of the board, handed down from one generation of directors to another, that only the classical and stylish type of player should be signed. The kick-and-rush type has never appealed to them."* Will Cuff

### MICK TELFER

1. Alex Young
2. Roy Vernon
3. Alan Ball
4. Gary Lineker
5. Neville Southall
6. Trevor Steven
7. Ray Wilson
8. Peter Reid
9. Jimmy Gabriel
10. Bob Latchford

*Everton fan*
*Maghull*

### DAVE WATSON

1. Neville Southall
2. Dixie Dean
3. Kevin Ratcliffe
4. Peter Reid
5. Graeme Sharp
6. Brian Labone
7. Trevor Steven
8. Kevin Sheedy
9. Howard Kendall
10. Colin Harvey

*Everton player*
*& coach*

### GORDON WEST

1. Brian Labone
2. Ray Wilson
3. Tony Kay
4. Alan Ball
5. Alex Young
6. Jimmy Gabriel
7. Howard Kendall
8. Colin Harvey
9. Tommy Wright
10. Alex Parker

*former-player*

### DON DONOVAN

1. Tommy Eglington
2. Peter Farrell
3. Ted Sagar
4. Eddie Wainwright
5. TG Jones
6. Wally Fielding
7. Jimmy O'Neill
8. Tommy Jones
9. Derek Temple
10. Brian Labone

*former-player*

### MICHAEL BALL

1. Neville Southall
2. Dixie Dean
3. Dave Watson
4. Gary Stevens
5. Trevor Steven
6. Pat Van den Hauwe
7. Kevin Ratcliffe
8. Kevin Sheedy
9. Andy Gray
10. Peter Reid

*Everton player*

### DAVE HOPKINS

1. Dave Watson
2. Graeme Sharp
3. Neville Southall
4. Howard Kendall
5. Peter Reid
6. Alan Ball
7. Kevin Sheedy
8. Joe Royle
9. Brian Labone
10. Ray Wilson

*matchday steward*

### PETER CLARKE

1. Neville Southall
2. Dave Watson
3. Dixie Dean
4. Andrei Kanchelskis
5. Bob Latchford
6. Colin Harvey
7. Brian Labone
8. Gary Stevens
9. Peter Reid
10. Alex Young

*Everton player*

Generations of blue-bloods have been raised on parables of Sharp and Makepeace at the turn of the century, Dean and Lawton in the 1930s, Young and Ball in the 1960s, Reid and Southall in the glory years …

### SIR PHILIP CARTER

1   Dixie Dean
2   Peter Farrell
3   Colin Harvey
4   Tommy Jones
5   Wally Fielding
6   Alan Ball
7   Johnny Morrissey
8   Dave Watson
9   Howard Kendall
10   Neville Southall

*Everton chairman*

### AUSTIN HEALEY

1   Trevor Steven
2   Kevin Campbell
3   Neville Southall
4   Andy Gray
5   Brian Labone
6   Tony Cottee
7   Kevin Ratcliffe
8   Kevin Sheedy
9   Peter Reid
10   Pat Van den Hauwe

*Leicester & England*
*Rugby Union*

### STEVE SEARGEANT

1   Dixie Dean
2   Bob Latchford
3   Roy Vernon
4   Alex Young
5   Ray Wilson
6   Alan Ball
7   Trevor Steven
8   Alex Parker
9   Brian Labone
10   Bobby Collins

*former-player*

### BILL DEAN

1   Dixie Dean
2   Warney Cresswell
3   Peter Farrell
4   Cliff Britton
5   Dennis Stevens
6   Jimmy Gabriel
7   Alex Parker
8   Howard Kendall
9   Alan Ball
10   Johnny Morrissey

*Brookside*

### FRANCIS JEFFERS

1   Andy Gray
2   Dixie Dean
3   Trevor Steven
4   Gary Lineker
5   Neville Southall
6   Andrei Kanchelskis
7   Colin Harvey
8   Howard Kendall
9   Bob Latchford
10   Peter Reid

*Everton player*

### DENIS O'MEARA

1   Alan Ball
2   Alex Young
3   Ray Wilson
4   Neville Southall
5   Colin Harvey
6   Peter Reid
7   Kevin Sheedy
8   Kevin Ratcliffe
9   Dave Hickson
10   Mike Lyons

*Everton fan*
*Hightown*

### JIMMY GABRIEL

1   Dixie Dean
2   Alex Young
3   Roy Vernon
4   Dave Hickson
5   Alan Ball
6   Brian Labone
7   Colin Harvey
8   Neville Southall
9   Howard Kendall
10   Joe Royle

*former-player*
*& coach*

### DAVID PRENTICE

1   Bob Latchford
2   Dixie Dean
3   Graeme Sharp
4   Neville Southall
5   Peter Reid
6   Dave Watson
7   Andy Gray
8   Gary Jones
9   Colin Todd
10   David Smallman

*Liverpool Echo*

### CHARLIE CROSBIE

1   Neville Southall
2   Alan Ball
3   Alex Young
4   Brian Labone
5   Jimmy Gabriel
6   Bobby Collins
7   Colin Harvey
8   Dave Watson
9   Bob Latchford
10   Duncan Ferguson

*Independent Blues*

*"No other club generates such lifelong affection. There is something regal about the hue of the blue shirts, the inspiration of the Latin motto, the legends of the School of Science, the aura of Goodison and the loyalty of the fans who follow the club around the world irrespective of Everton's playing fortunes."* Alex Young

### RICHARD LEWIS

| | |
|---|---|
| 1 | Alan Ball |
| 2 | Neville Southall |
| 3 | Alex Young |
| 4 | Ray Wilson |
| 5 | Joe Royle |
| 6 | Howard Kendall |
| 7 | Peter Reid |
| 8 | Graeme Sharp |
| 9 | Brian Labone |
| 10 | Kevin Ratcliffe |

*Everton Shareholders'
Association*

### JIMMY HARRIS

| | |
|---|---|
| 1 | Dixie Dean |
| 2 | Bobby Collins |
| 3 | Brian Labone |
| 4 | Roy Vernon |
| 5 | Ray Wilson |
| 6 | Brian Harris |
| 7 | Alex Parker |
| 8 | Alan Ball |
| 9 | Neville Southall |
| 10 | Peter Reid |

*former-player*

### MARTIN DOBSON

| | |
|---|---|
| 1 | Dixie Dean |
| 2 | Brian Labone |
| 3 | Neville Southall |
| 4 | Ted Sagar |
| 5 | Ray Wilson |
| 6 | Howard Kendall |
| 7 | Alex Young |
| 8 | Joe Royle |
| 9 | Trevor Steven |
| 10 | Dave Hickson |

*former-player*

### TOM EGGLESTON

| | |
|---|---|
| 1 | Brian Labone |
| 2 | Colin Harvey |
| 3 | Alex Young |
| 4 | Alan Ball |
| 5 | Howard Kendall |
| 6 | Jimmy Gabriel |
| 7 | Alex Scott |
| 8 | Ray Wilson |
| 9 | Joe Royle |
| 10 | Gordon West |

*former-coach*

### ALAN WHITTLE

| | |
|---|---|
| 1 | Ray Wilson |
| 2 | Alan Ball |
| 3 | Tony Kay |
| 4 | Brian Labone |
| 5 | Alex Young |
| 6 | Colin Harvey |
| 7 | Johnny Morrissey |
| 8 | Howard Kendall |
| 9 | Bob Latchford |
| 10 | Graeme Sharp |

*former-player*

### STAN BENTHAM

| | |
|---|---|
| 1 | Dixie Dean |
| 2 | Ted Sagar |
| 3 | Joe Mercer |
| 4 | TG Jones |
| 5 | Alex Stevenson |
| 6 | Tommy Lawton |
| 7 | Brian Labone |
| 8 | Tommy Eglington |
| 9 | Dave Hickson |
| 10 | Peter Farrell |

*former-player
& coach*

### BRYAN HAMILTON

| | |
|---|---|
| 1 | Alan Ball |
| 2 | Dixie Dean |
| 3 | Joe Mercer |
| 4 | Alex Young |
| 5 | Roy Vernon |
| 6 | Ray Wilson |
| 7 | Joe Royle |
| 8 | Colin Harvey |
| 9 | Howard Kendall |
| 10 | Bobby Collins |

*former-player*

Even though the club has struggled to maintain its footballing traditions,
Evertonians have never lost their appetite for rich, flowing football ...

### BILL KENWRIGHT
1. Dave Hickson
2. Roy Vernon
3. Alex Young
4. Alan Ball
5. Howard Kendall
6. Bobby Collins
7. Brian Labone
8. Duncan McKenzie
9. Neville Southall
10. Jimmy Gabriel

*Everton deputy-chairman*

### NEVILLE SOUTHALL
1. Dixie Dean
2. Brian Labone
3. Dave Hickson
4. Alan Ball
5. Colin Harvey
6. Howard Kendall
7. Ted Sagar
8. Bob Latchford
9. Kevin Ratcliffe
10. Mike Lyons

*former-player*

### NORMAN JONES
1. Alex Young
2. Dixie Dean
3. Brian Labone
4. TG Jones
5. Dave Hickson
6. Graeme Sharp
7. Neville Southall
8. Joe Mercer
9. Bobby Collins
10. Howard Kendall

*Everton fan*
*Liverpool*

### MARK OWEN
1. Duncan McKenzie
2. Peter Reid
3. Andy King
4. Graeme Sharp
5. Alan Ball
6. Neville Southall
7. Pat Nevin
8. Alan Harper
9. Kevin Campbell
10. Joe Harper

*Granada TV*

### ANDY KING
1. Neville Southall
2. Pater Reid
3. Bob Latchford
4. Andy Gray
5. Colin Harvey
6. Kevin Ratcliffe
7. Dave Thomas
8. Trevor Steven
9. Mike Pejic
10. Francis Jeffers

*former-player*

### NICK BARMBY
1. Peter Beardsley
2. Alan Ball
3. Colin Harvey
4. Neville Southall
5. Gary Lineker
6. Andrei Kanchelskis
7. Trevor Steven
8. Dixie Dean
9. Brian Labone
10. Dave Hickson

*Everton player*

### SANDY BROWN
1. Alex Young
2. Brian Labone
3. Alan Ball
4. Gordon West
5. Ray Wilson
6. Tony Kay
7. Colin Harvey
8. Howard Kendall
9. Alex Scott
10. Dennis Stevens

*former-player*

### MARK TALLENTIRE
1. Bob Latchford
2. Graeme Sharp
3. Kevin Ratcliffe
4. Martin Dobson
5. George Wood
6. Mike Lyons
7. Gary Jones
8. Trevor Steven
9. Alan Whittle
10. Tony Cottee

*The Guardian*

### NORMAN CROTTY
1. Alex Young
2. Trevor Steven
3. Fred Pickering
4. Alex Parker
5. Bob Latchford
6. Ray Wilson
7. Alan Ball
8. Roy Vernon
9. Peter Farrell
10. Dave Hickson

*Bellefield security*

*"I think that we are special! It's true that during the past decade we have not had an awful lot of joy, but we continue our proud record of having played more games in the top flight than any other club and long for the return of the years of glory."* Bill Kenwright

### GLYN TUDOR

1 Neville Southall
2 Dixie Dean
3 Bob Latchford
4 Dave Watson
5 Gary Lineker
6 Ray Wilson
7 Howard Kendall
8 Brian Labone
9 Peter Reid
10 Gary Speed

*Everton fan*
*Buckley*

### FRED PICKERING

1 Tommy Lawton
2 Roy Vernon
3 Alan Ball
4 Alex Parker
5 Ray Wilson
6 Jimmy Gabriel
7 Gordon West
8 Brian Labone
9 Johnny Morrissey
10 Alex Scott

*former-player*

### GORDON WATSON

1 Dixie Dean
2 Tommy Lawton
3 Joe Mercer
4 Ted Sagar
5 Billy Cook
6 Cliff Britton
7 TG Jones
8 Alex Young
9 Alex Stevenson
10 Torry Gillick

*former-player*
*& coach*

### DEREK MOUNTFIELD

1 Bob Latchford
2 Neville Southall
3 Trevor Steven
4 Martin Dobson
5 Peter Reid
6 Graeme Sharp
7 Mike Lyons
8 Duncan McKenzie
9 Andy King
10 Kevin Sheedy

*former-player*

### ALEX YOUNG

1 Alan Ball
2 Roy Vernon
3 Tony Kay
4 Tommy Lawton
5 Dixie Dean
6 Bobby Collins
7 Neville Southall
8 Gordon West
9 Peter Reid
10 Ray Wilson

*former-player*

### JIMMY O'NEILL

1 Neville Southall
2 Brian Labone
3 Peter Farrell
4 Tommy Eglington
5 Howard Kendall
6 Alan Ball
7 Ray Wilson
8 Gordon West
9 Peter Reid
10 Trevor Steven

*former-player*

### MARK McVEY

1 Andy Gray
2 Dixie Dean
3 Neville Southall
4 Dave Watson
5 Howard Kendall
6 Alan Ball
7 Alex Young
8 Nick Barmby
9 Trevor Steven
10 Kevin Campbell

*retail manager*

For some, marriage to a football club is no longer a word - it is a sentence. A few members of the royal blue fraternity weaned on cynicism and woe have proposed a Park End Hall of Shame or something similar ...

### HALL OF SHAME CANDIDATES

| | |
|---|---|
| 1 | Brett Angell |
| 2 | Rod Belfitt |
| 3 | Ibrahima Bakayoko |
| 4 | Bernie Wright |
| 5 | Alan Biley |
| 6 | Glenn Keeley |
| 7 | Micky Walsh |
| 8 | Marc Hottiger |
| 9 | Neil McDonald |
| 10 | Claus Thomsen |
| 11 | John McLaughlin |
| 12 | Stefan Rehn |

### UNPRODUCTIVE PURCHASES

| | |
|---|---|
| 1 | Slaven Bilic |
| 2 | Mo Johnston |
| 3 | Ibrahima Bakayoko |
| 4 | John Spencer |
| 5 | Danny Williamson |
| 6 | Rod Belfitt |
| 7 | Vinnie Samways |
| 8 | Micky Walsh |
| 9 | Marc Hottiger |
| 10 | David Lawson |
| 11 | Claus Thomsen |
| 12 | Terry Phelan |

### PREMIER BAD BOYS

| | |
|---|---|
| 1 | Duncan Ferguson |
| 2 | Slaven Bilic |
| 3 | David Unsworth |
| 4 | Olivier Dacourt |
| 5 | Don Hutchison |
| 6 | Marco Materazzi |
| 7 | Barry Horne |
| 8 | Richard Dunne |
| 9 | Dave Watson |
| 10 | John Ebbrell |
| 11 | Joe Parkinson |
| 12 | Craig Short |

### UNFORTUNATE POST-WAR BLUNDERS

| | | | | |
|---|---|---|---|---|
| 1 | Gary Stevens | May 10, 1986 | wayward pass | Liverpool |
| 2 | Anders Limpar | May 7, 1994 | handball | Wimbledon |
| 3 | Glenn Keeley | November 6, 1982 | sent off | Liverpool |
| 4 | Sandy Brown | December 6, 1969 | own goal | Liverpool |
| 5 | Duncan Ferguson | February 14, 1998 | sent off | Derby County |
| 6 | Tommy Clinton | March 21, 1953 | missed penalty | Bolton Wanderers |
| 7 | Nick Barmby | May 10, 1999 | missed penalty | Coventry City |
| 8 | Terry Darracott | April 13, 1977 | missed tackle | Aston Villa |
| 9 | Slaven Bilic | March 7, 1998 | sent off | Southampton |
| 10 | Jimmy Husband | May 18, 1968 | missed goal | West Bromwich Albion |
| 11 | Duncan McKenzie | February 15, 1977 | missed penalty | Bolton Wanderers |
| 12 | Mike Lyons | October 20, 1979 | own goal | Liverpool |